Hey Roberto Hu

About the author:

Matthias Leue is a Benicia, California-based writer, fine art photographer, watercolor artist, and kids cooking class instructor, who also loves to cook and eat!

Born in Köln, Germany, he moved back and forth between Germany and the United States several times, living in Philadelphia, Frankfurt, on the Monterey Peninsula, and all over the San Francisco Bay Area.

He received his B.F.A. in Photography from the San Francisco Art Institute in 1980.

Hey, Roberto Hu is his third published book.

Other Books by Matthias Leue

Fish Camping and Other Travel Stories

Sea Shells, C'est Gratuit

Hey Roberto Hu

Matthias Leue

First Edition, May, 2021

© 2021 by Matthias Leue

Published by Flatfish Books
Benicia, California
www.flatfish-books.com

Palm tree and swordfish drawing: Patrick Leue
Author photo: Gary Hunt
Editor: Sarah Holroyd, Sleeping Cat Books
Watercolors and book design: Matthias Leue

ISBN 13: 978-0-9835351-3-3

Library of Congress Control Number: 2020912757

Library of Congress subject headings:
United States -- Description and travel, humor
Travelers' writings
Special Interest, adventure
Venezuela
South America
Northwest, Pacific -- Description and travel, humor

About this book:

Hey, Roberto Hu is my third published book. The title is taken from the first story in the book: a visit to the exotic country of Venezuela, a journey that I never imagined I would take during my lifetime. My youngest son, Patrick, spent a year after college in Venezuela teaching English, cooking in several restaurants, and studying on a Fulbright scholarship. I did not want to miss this once-in-a-lifetime opportunity to visit him, and it turned out to be a fascinating trip. I feel so blessed not only to have experienced but to have been able to photograph Venezuela—or a small portion of it, I should say—and the incredibly varied and often totally new to me landscapes. Photography has always been one of my passions in life. I hope the story will allow the reader to experience a small slice of this equatorial country.

Some of my other passions include writing and watercolors. I have dreamed about, then planned, and eventually started to write a cookbook to include some drawings by my sons, with my watercolors as well as photos. This desire dates back to our beginning culinary days in a tiny San Francisco apartment in the early 90s, where I first taught my young sons how to cook. The cookbook is still a work in progress, and I hope that it will become a family treasure in the future.

I had longed to take up photography once again, a field in which I had received my BFA degree in 1980, shortly before my first son, Christian, was born. I had completed a portfolio of black and white images of craftsmen and farmers in a rural part of Germany, with August Sander as an inspiration, which were part of the graduation exhibit at my school. I had to shelve photography after I finished school, however, as I couldn't get a job in the field, save for a very short stint processing film and a couple of other commercial projects, which were not only frustrating to me but also infrequent and with poor compensation. I ended up driving a taxi for decades to support my family. In 2006 I finally went back to school part-time for several semesters on some grants and took some classes to make the switch from analog to digital photography, and then applied this new-found knowledge in creating portfolios for an open studio in my loft in Oakland, where I was then able to display my impressions of Venezuela. I absolutely loved my loft. Since losing my home in 1988 I'd spent over a decade surviving and moving from place to place before I found this place to rent. I had just come back from a family visit with my sons to Germany in the summer of 2001 (they had returned a few weeks earlier) with no place to live again. After spending a depressing few nights in a motel, I moved back into a tiny room above my church, where I had slept for several weeks prior to the visit to Germany. After finally talking to, and telling the senior pastor of the church about my living situation—he was shocked I was living in the room there—we then prayed together for me to find a place to live. Our prayer was answered the next day in the form of rental listing I found in the newspaper for my loft. The owners, Tom and Anita, lived next door to it and were willing to accept me as a tenant.

Prior to my continued photo education, my sons had both left for college—the last one in 2002, I tried to fill the single-parent empty-nest time by taking some classes at a community college: first a woodworking class, where I built a small table, and then some ceramics classes. Both of these tactile classes were inspiring and fun, especially the ceramics classes where I was able to draw and paint again. I also started working on some new drawings and watercolors to enhance family travel stories that I had written and collected over the years with the intent of turning them into books, and as something to pass on later. Some of these stories and watercolors appear in my prior books, the first of which was published in 2012. Good things really do take time, and it has been fun to watch things come together over the decades. Holding that first published, printed book was really special. In a way, books are like your kids.

At this point my cat, Calvin—a God-sent gift—who came to me as a three-month-old kitten in the summer of 2009, wishes to intercede: Calvin here: why yes, funny you should ask, I will be glad to chime in. The author sure is a chatterbox. I was, if I may humbly say so, an adorable kitten, although I must also state with some trepidation that I was a "trade-in" for my sister who, prior to my arrival in my caretaker's loft, hid and whined under his bed for an entire night before she was brought back to the litter of which I was a part, clearing the path for my arrival. My sister was a bit on the whiney side, but then again she was younger than me and wasn't quite ready to depart yet. Obviously I should have been the first choice, but all is forgiven as my caretaker explained that he originally chose my sister because of her light gray color. Why, you ask? Well, my caretaker had a cat prior to me named Hobbes, who was hit by a reckless driver about three or four months prior to my coming into this home. My caretaker was extremely sad when this happened as he loved Hobbes very much. Incidentally Hobbes and I have the same mother—but we are of course from a different litter. I must interrupt myself at this point and wish to say that "litter" is rather a poor choice of words for my brothers and sisters as well as myself—it conjures up images of untidiness, and we are not! To come back to my original train of thought though: my coloration and markings are indeed very, very similar to my predecessor Hobbes, and my caretaker told me that's the reason why he first chose my sister, because he didn't want to be reminded of Hobbes, as he was still sad. So there you have it in a nutshell.

Now admittedly, it was a bit scary for me to be in a new place, but crying and whining under the bed all night long, as was the case with my sister... well, that's a bit silly, if you ask me. Upon arrival I was treated to some milk, a rather tasty something that smelled like chicken in a clean bowl set out for me, and there was an additional bowl filled with crunchies. What's not to like? Then I was allowed to sleep in my caretaker's bed. Oh my, I have never felt anything so soft! Naturally I missed my family a bit and cried some, but I felt that this was someone who loved me and would take care of me. So, a few more whimpers on my behalf and then I happily drifted off to sleep in a cozy blanket.

I was already familiar with and started to use a litter box set out for me right away, much to my caretaker's delight—my mother had taught me—but soon after arriving I seldom used this box, as the beautiful yard and forest outside the loft allowed me to take care of business properly without the unpleasant fumes from a litter box. These new quarters were lovely: lots of windows with sunlight streaming through them, so sunny spots to sleep in, plenty of good food and tasty tidbits as already mentioned, an exquisite place to sleep, and lots of petting whenever I was so inclined.

I also very quickly learned to retrieve a stuffed mouse, as well as a stuffed hedgehog—actually there were two: one small one, and one hedgehog larger than myself—which had belonged to Hobbes, and to carry said critters up the stairs and lay them at my caretaker's feet. He would respond by calling me a good boy, petting my head, and then, while making some kind of whistling sound, he would toss the mouse, or hedgehog as the case may be, back down the stairs for me to retrieve once again. I usually would do this four or five times in a row, so afterwards I was often winded, especially with the hedgehog that was larger than myself.

I learned that my predecessor Hobbes had been quite a character: he would check both doors of the loft—front and back—when he wanted to come in. If that didn't work, he would then hop on the windowsill outside of the kitchen window and meow as long as it took to get inside. Persistent fellow, if I may say so. Apparently he enjoyed unusual places to sleep too: once in the dryer (the door had been left open), occasionally in a laundry basket, and once in a dresser drawer that had not been closed properly. When he did sleep in bed, he would spend the entire night in one position under the blanket, never moving once. Personally I feel a bit suffocated that way and prefer to sleep next to the pillow of my caretaker.

I was told Hobbes once sat on a chair at the dining table and gently and politely ate a few pieces of Dungeness crab from a small plate that was placed in front of him without putting either of his paws on the table. I am rather fond of Dungeness crab myself, and although I have not eaten at the table, my dining habits are equally as good, if I may humbly say so.

I started to grow in size, in weight, and in learning. I have remained small in stature, however, but as it is said, "good things come in small packages." I am an excellent hunter, by the way, and my caretaker was much surprised when I once caught a loud and rather irritating blue jay for lunch. Lunch was bigger than me in size and after showing my prey to my caretaker I then very quickly darted off into the forest—sorry, no sharing that prize. I am also able to understand several words in other languages, my favorite being the Spanish word pescado (fish). My caretaker occasionally likes to brag a bit of the fact that I comprehend over 50 different words. Obviously my favorite ones are food related.

Having acclimated to my new surroundings I was contemplating a relaxed life here in this charming loft with such an abundance of nature all around us. It really was quite lovely here. One of our neighbors, Bill is his name, with whom I came to spend time later on during my caretaker's excursions, was always up early. I would either watch him from an upstairs window or sometimes follow him when he retrieved his morning newspaper if the back door was open, and it often was—just wide enough for me to slip out. My caretaker is somewhat unfamiliar with the term "morning," I do believe, and he keeps rather odd hours.

The years 2009 and 2010 were difficult. I had to comfort my caretaker quite a bit, which I gladly did, of course, as he lost first his mom in 2009, and then his dad the following year. Then my caretaker had to go to some place called a hospital. He was dormant for a while after that and his bed was moved downstairs close to his and my (occasional use) restroom. I also got to meet his two sons, Christian and Patrick, and although I tend not to be too fond of being called "kitty" or "small cat" by said sons on occasion, I rather do like them both. They helped my caretaker a lot, something I was of course unable to do due to my limitations, you understand. I will take a deserved short break here now and let my caretaker continue to ramble for a bit before I chime in again later once more.

Author here: Having had back surgery in the spring of 2010, it took me a while to recuperate, but in late fall, I was able to visit my old friends Patrick (who is now in heaven) and Sanae up in Portland, a lovely and vibrant city where my youngest son, Patrick, and his girlfriend, Hannah, now have a home, a place which I have always considered somewhat of a second home. "Ten Minutes or Thirty Years" is the story that came out of that trip to the Pacific Northwest. I also got to know Hannah, whom I met in the summer of 2009, a little bit better. She is a kind and warm-hearted girl. I had hoped and prayed for a long time for God to give Patrick someone like her to hopefully have a family with. They have been practicing — first with an African hedgehog named Marlin who has since departed to hedgehog heaven, and then with a coop full of ducks and a lovely cat named Pierre who sadly passed away recently. That was very hard for Patrick and Hannah, as well as for Calvin and me.

""The Gold Panner at Maxwell" and "Right Side, Left Side" are two stories about small excursions in California. The first is about a visit to Redding, where one of my photos was chosen for an exhibit at the Turtle Bay Exploration Park. The latter is about a trip to hear some beloved Brazilian musicians who were playing at Kuumbwa Jazz Center in Santa Cruz.

"Schnukiputzi Turns French" and "Cat Carriers" are stories about visits to Portland and its vicinity to see my family and friends. It is visits like this that help to keep me going.

Calvin here again: my much anticipated and envisioned life in and around the loft was not to be, however, although I had four lovely years in Oakland after my arrival in 2009. In 2013 my caretaker and I were forced to move to a town called Benicia by the rather unpleasant person who owned the loft we resided in. I'm still a bit unclear about property and such, as those things really tend not to be part of my daily concerns.

The unexpected arrival in our Benicia apartment unfortunately included harassment by a dim-witted brute known as the "junk yard cat" who made my life miserable on occasion when he came around, although I found places to hide outside that the overweight savage—twice my size—could not get into. My caretaker defended me valiantly whenever he saw the miscreant by use of thrown small objects in the brute's direction or by use of the water hose, which usually facilitated a hasty retreat with the occasional direct hit, much to my satisfaction. The brute got to know my caretaker by sight, which acted as a deterrent.

My other pet peeve was the obnoxious wiener dog next door, who at the slightest noise or provocation would go into a barking frenzy. A hysteric imbecile—so much fuss about nothing. Then, a few years later, a batch of Chihuahuas occupied the apartment right next to ours—an unending nightmare—but I digress.

I was able to take walks down the stairs from the apartment to a courtyard in the back to which my caretaker had moved all his potted plants, and I was also able to take walks in a little alley behind the courtyard, albeit always somewhat on the defensive because of the possibility of encountering you-know-who. I seldom ventured in the direction of the carport as I don't like cars, which was also a big relief for my caretaker. But this is really quite another story, and if I can get my caretaker to get up somewhat earlier in the day, perhaps he can expand on the move and trying to adapt to our new habitat in another book after this one—there is much to be told.

Author here again: hint taken; I'm working on it. I shall ignore the snide remark about my concept of "morning," as well as those little "ramble" and "chatterbox" quips. A treat may, or may not, be served today in regards to that little misstep.

Matthias Leue

Holger: Love you, bro, and thank you for your reliability.

Thank you to Pastor and Linda Holt for their warmth.

Gary: I miss you my true friend.

Thank you, God, for leading this doofus on the long journey home.

Story Index

Hey Roberto Hu

Hey, Roberto Hu
May 2007

San Francisco Airport, late May of 2007. I'm off to Caracas, Venezuela to visit my son Patrick, with two stopovers: Miami and San Juan, Puerto Rico. The Bay Area lights sparkle below on this night flight as the flight attendant brings some cheese and fruit, including dried dates, on my mileage redemption excursion in business class. I think it took me more than a decade to accumulate the miles. I feel fortunate to be able to stretch my legs out. The pilot wakes the cabin with his announcement that Houston is directly below us, a piece of information that most of us could safely have lived without, I tend to think. Perhaps he resides there and is homesick.

Pre-dawn, 5 a.m. We land in Miami. It's a 20-minute walk to the next terminal, which leads me to conclude that this is an airport of quite some size. Newly restored, this terminal has a multitude of fish replicas in bright colors arranged in circular patterns on the wall: bonitos, opahs, sailfish, tuna, sharks—an amusing collection of sea dwellers. I wander to the restroom, where I see a guy washing underwear in the sink. No laundromat? Business interview? I don't think I want to know the full story this early in the morning.

The first workers are sluggishly making their way through the terminal. As I await the flight to San Juan, a few Spanish-speaking people chat or glance at the clock periodically. There is some really annoying loud jazz music playing in the background. Why? I love jazz, but it is 5 a.m. Can't Americans ever have just quiet? I glance at a huge puffy white cloud outside that looks like a sea horse. Outside another window, a puddle under an aircraft reflects the

BONITO

slowly dawning shrimp- and amber-colored light.

An omelet brightens the next leg of the journey to San Juan, Puerto Rico, and another brief nap follows. My ears signal that we are about to land. Opening the sunshade of the "porthole" lets in the bright Caribbean sun. Looking out as the plane makes its descent into San Juan Airport, I notice a cruise ship docked in the harbor, and houses painted in bright Caribbean colors such as one sees in travel brochures.

The airport terminal in San Juan could be anywhere in the U.S., except for the fact that there are some Puerto Rican food specialty stores. I walk around the terminal to pass the time before the next flight, as there is not enough time to pay a visit to the city of San Juan. Looking out of one of the windows, I see some ancient prop planes parked near a hangar, another indication that we are indeed outside the U.S.—although technically, Puerto Rico is a U.S. territory, for those who object. I opt for another short nap in my chair at the gate, tired after the night flight.

The last flight segment now, to Venezuela. I doze off again. Waking up and peering through the window, I see the ocean below us in incredible turquoise and azure hues. As it turns out, the scene below will later be one of Patrick's and my destinations: Los Roques National Park off the coast of Caracas. The sun is incredibly bright here at the equator. On the final descent into Caracas airport, high-rise apartments and an industrial landscape composed of warehouses, car wrecking yards, and patches of arid land appear on the ground below. Certainly not what I expected, especially in that combination.

The customs form has an outline of the shape of the country of Venezuela on it, and is, of course, *en español*. Immigration is located in a brand new terminal that is air conditioned. The inspector is formal and polite as he views and stamps my German passport. I walk through the doors and see Patrick, smiling and bronzed from the sun. After a big hug, we start to look for a rental car. We encounter a few unsavory types offering currency exchange services (which Patrick had warned me to avoid). Ignoring them, and after searching and some discussion at various rental agency counters, we finally find a rental car: a dark blue Toyota Yaris. I most definitely want the insurance coverage—a smart but controversial decision, as we will find out later.

Outside the terminal, it is incredibly hot. Oleander and bougainvillea grow like weeds. I'm here! In South America! I still can't believe it. We start the long drive along the only route into Caracas. Perched on the hills, red brick shacks and ramshackle abodes are crammed together, with palms dotting the landscape in between. Patrick informs me that many of these homes have no running water or electricity. Caracas is a city of economic extremes. I spot a yellow Twingo, the first I have seen outside Europe. What fun to see one of my favorite modes of transportation. Want to trade for a Yaris? A large billboard picturing Hugo Chávez wearing a red beret and shirt, fist raised in the air, stands prominently on the side of the road. "He is all over Venezuela," Patrick tells me. The mountain road winds onward with heavy traffic. (A new bridge is being built to help thin out traffic, but it will probably still take many years to be completed). It is stop-and-go for many miles.

Finally we arrive in Caracas, and Patrick directs me toward a hotel he has chosen for me. He says he will stay the first night with me rather than return to his host family, to keep me company. In staying true to my primary occupation as a taxi driver I make an illegal left turn, right in front of a pretty traffic cop, to head down the street to our hotel. As it turns out, the so-called illegal turn is pretty much de facto here — but more on that later. The hotel has gated parking, and we manage to squeeze the Yaris into the tiny lot. After checking in and taking the elevator upstairs, we unpack, relax, chat, and then nap for a while.

After dark, we walk outside to get dinner. What a carnivore's delight Patrick has chosen! Inside is what looks like a glass display case but is, in fact, a refrigerator, with various cuts of beef hung on meat hooks, and there are more steaks at the base of it. The walls of the restaurant are paneled in dark wood, with old oil paintings. A classic steak house motif, but with a South America flair. After a crab bisque, we have steaks, of course, with yucca and fries on the side, accompanied by a fine red wine.

We leave the restaurant and take a stroll into the plaza of the Altamira district. We pass a fountain, and rocks with water flowing over a steep edge and plummeting down at least one story. Patrick

BOU GAINVILLEA

thinks it's a good idea to drop off my suitcase at his host family's house for safekeeping, as we won't take it on our trip tomorrow. We drive there and park at a gate in front of the high-rise building. After Patrick operates the key to unlock the elevator, we ascend to the penthouse and drop off the suitcase. On the terrace below us is a magnificent nighttime view. Thousands of lights twinkle and sparkle over Caracas. We return to my hotel and squeeze the Yaris back into its resting place.

There are only sheets on the beds for cover, but they are more than adequate, as it is still hot. Shortly after midnight the garbage trucks decide to go to work—nice timing, gentlemen. After this interruption, we fall asleep again. At dawn, I hear someone barking instructions over a megaphone. Are you kidding me? Then I hear the sound of kids running and playing and some girls chanting,

FRUIT STAND, CARACAS, VENEZUELA

"Hey, Roberto Hu." Looking out the window, I see a school, with boys playing soccer and girls cheering on the side for Roberto, who seems adept at playing ball. I turn around to hear Patrick remark, "Roberto's the man." Forget about sleeping in, so we shower, if the trickle coming out of the shower head may be called that.

We leave the hotel, and Patrick invites me for some small eclairs and coffee in a bakery. Emerging from the cafe, I am amazed to see so many buildings with gates and bars in front of the windows, and often barbed wire on top of the walls—like a prison in a movie. I guess it's because of the extremes of poverty and riches. Still, what a way to live; who are the prisoners here? We see a spot to park near a produce truck. The proprietor has set up a stand and we choose from the assortment of tropical fruits on display, buying fresh, juicy mangos. I photograph an incredible-looking tree whose roots have completely overgrown a foundation and wall—hanging at least five feet over the wall. Take that, civilization! Think concrete will stop me? Think again!

I have seen various types of taxis pass us on the streets (professional curiosity). Patrick tells me about the many gypsy taxis here, which basically operate like this: some guy walks into a store and prints up a sticker that says "Taxi" on it and slaps it on the side of his car. Ready to go. To be hired with caution, to say the least.

As we walk down a street near the hotel, Patrick points and says, "Look!" I look ahead but see nothing. "Look again." Mango trees! I am dumbstruck. The first mango tree I have ever seen—with an abundance of green mangos hanging from it. This country is fascinating! What a sight!

For lunch we have some *reina pepiada arepas*, a Venezuelan corn-flour bread with chicken salad, and *capresa*, a type of tomato salad. Our next stop is at a botanical garden, but it's closed, so we decide to walk around the perimeter in the beautiful afternoon light. I am taking lots of pictures of shadow and light in what photographers call the "golden light," and I wonder why Patrick is often across the street watching me. He says, "Oh, I'm just keeping an eye out for you." I guess in my excitement to be here, and ignorance of the ways of the country, I don't really take crime as seriously as he does. Such a thoughtful son. (Recently, after returning home, I read that Venezuela has over 23,000 murders a year—some as petty as over a pair of shoes—a frightening statistic.)

Diving into the late-afternoon car chaos, we drive to the restaurant that Patrick is working at part-time. (I have always loved the kitchens of restaurants: the smells, the activity, and the excitement. I guess it started with watching my friend Big Patrick cook in his Italian restaurant in Portland, Oregon.) An interesting sight: a wall on one side of the kitchen, covered top to bottom with bright white tiles, is used for communication, with instructions, inventory, etc. written on it. Great functional use of objects—unless someone with an eraser comes along, of course. I get to sample a parmesan tart, and am given a jar of passion fruit jam. *Gracias*!

We then drive to Patrick's language school, to pick up some shoes he has forgotten there, which he is planning to wear for an embassy dinner sponsored by the school. On the way back I let Patrick drive and, confound it, a tree jumps out right in front of him, denting Mr. Yaris. I'm glad I bought the insurance.

Arriving at the home of Patrick's host family, I meet Toby, the man of the house. The inside of the penthouse is an assault on the senses, albeit a positive one. The walls are covered with paintings, and there are sculptures and carvings, bromeliads and orchids everywhere; a museum would pale in comparison. The sound of tree frogs can be heard outside. Patrick then finds out that the embassy dinner is canceled, so we decide to meet his friend Dorothy for dinner in Patrick's restaurant: superb small pizza as the main course and an exotic juice drink to go with it. We head home to my hotel for the night and go to sleep, as we will be on the road tomorrow.

After packing the next morning, we have to get the keys from the front desk to unlock the gate to retrieve our Yaris, as we are the first ones up this early in the morning. After a few detours, we find the general direction to Mérida, our intended destination. Patrick is more familiar with walking or using the buses in Caracas, so it takes him a bit of time to get his bearings in a car. We pull off at an exit and stop at a bakery to get some breakfast. Numerous *perros de la calle*, or street dogs, are loitering or sleeping near the entrance hoping for a handout or a dropped morsel, probably attracted by the sweet smells drifting from the bakery. Members of the Venezuelan army are directing traffic at a plaza, an unfamiliar sight to me. Another wrong turn, as we seem to be in a market area. I see a truck fully loaded with plantains, an intriguing sight. The early commute traffic increases. Finally we make it to the right road. It is a mountainous descent from Caracas with trees blooming in many unfamiliar colors,: orange, pink, purple, lavender, and red, with incredibly lush vegetation.

Patrick is tired and decides to nap while I keep driving. I chuckle to see a pickup truck with two big ornate chairs fit for an emperor in the back of the truck and guys sitting in them. I also see a 50-foot-tall building in the shape of a juice carton: oversized, but certainly effective advertising. Much later, I pull off at a gas station to fill up. It costs me the equivalent of 90 cents to fill up the tank! I think the plantain chips that Patrick buys cost more. They are better than any potato chips I have tasted, but just as addictive, and then gone, as you can't just eat one. Hibiscus bushes surround the gas station, attesting to the fact that we are in a tropical climate.

At Maracay we must have made a wrong turn, and after consulting the map we turn around to head north. There are several construction zones, and rather than having a worker there, they have a mechanical guy or scarecrow dressed as a highway construction worker waving a flag. Probably a much safer way to go, but amusing nonetheless and unexpected—better on the payroll too, I expect. We get stopped at one of the numerous checkpoints, and a brutish cop starts to bark at Patrick. I have made the mistake of leaving my camera in view on my lap, and he probably figures he can make some easy money. Thank God Patrick speaks Spanish. The cop argues with us about having incorrect insurance (which is not true) and about Patrick driving the car, as the car is in my name, trying to find any excuse he can to arrest us. He is ready to impound the car and put us in jail unless we pay a fine. Patrick manages to get him to reduce the amount of the fine, but we still end up paying about $70 for him to let us go; probably a month's salary for the swine. Rolling up the windows, we depart, fuming at the injustice, expressing our wish that his dog bites him, and that his wife, if he has one—which is doubtful—runs away with the mailman. Up north on the coast is the town of Morón, which we decide must certainly be named after him.

The coast is dotted with refineries, an ugly sight. We stop to buy a better map (a colorful and very pretty one) and credits for the phone. Slowly our anger about our checkpoint experience dissipates -- we won't let this incident ruin our trip. The newly-built divided road is beautiful, with bougainvillea in all colors growing everywhere on the expansive median, the surrounding grass trimmed short to show off the bougainvillea. Suddenly, on the median, I see a parrot sales-man! He waves at us. He has two parrots, one on his shoulder and one on his arm. I surely would have bought one if I lived here.

A billboard advertises a botanical garden in the town of San Felipe,

PARROT - VENEZUELA   ©2012

so we opt for a detour, as we both love plants and gardens. It turns out to be nonexistent, though, so we turn around. Up ahead is another checkpoint; this time it's an army checkpoint and we panic, remembering our last experience. I'm driving, and the camera is out of sight, but I'm sweating. I try a new technique, avoiding eye contact on approach and feigning interest in the other side of the road. It seems to work; we are waved through. A sigh of relief.

We make a pit stop in Barquisimeto, one of the stadium sites for the

COPA 2007, or South American Soccer Cup, which Venezuela is hosting this year. It is only a month away, and they are still trying to finish building several stadiums in Venezuela. We see a giant—it may be inflated—plastic parrot advertising the COPA, his tail feathers in the colors of the Venezuelan flag. From what can be seen from the car, the town is an ugly, dirty industrial wasteland. For *almuerzo*, or lunch if you prefer, we have *pollo*: chicken. The restaurant, which is mostly outside, has several cages filled with birds, some of them parrots. Diesel fumes and truck noise surround us. Poor birds, not only caged but subjected to such foul air.

Happy to leave here, we now ascend roads on a mountain that gradually becomes a partial desert. On the descent, trees slowly appear again. Passing through a valley, I spot thick, black, billowy clouds of smoke on the left. Coming to a sudden stop, we see burning sugar cane fields, bright orange flames leaping sky high, behind trucks loaded with long cane stalks. A fascinating and rather

eerie sight. What an unbelievable variety of landscape thus far! A long stretch of bright red rock formations ranging in color from carmine to vermilion to almost sockeye salmon follows. As far as the road is concerned, some insane passing maneuvers are going on here, seemingly with no regard to curves or road width; I am stunned by the utter recklessness.

We reach the town of Valera and decide to stop for the night. It's dusk and it has been a long day. We find a decently priced hotel and check in. We have a scotch and soda and a hotel dinner, then head to our room. I have a long, fun talk with Patrick about life. It has been a while since we have had a chance to talk so much together since he left for college and then went on scholarship to Venezuela after graduating. I am so proud of him. Outside, the noise of boom-boxes can be heard, but we are both too tired to care anymore after the long eventful day, and just doze off.

Early morning again, and after a stroll up the street we find a small shop with large coffees, pastries, and water bottles for the road. Patrick chit-chats with the owner for a bit before our drive up into the mountains. The landscape is totally different again today, still with many bougainvillea and other colorful flowers, but also with lush green fields, carefully planted along the mountain slopes, utilizing the terrain to the maximum. I take some photos of what I think are a type of blackbird sitting in a field of artichokes—which I did not expect to grow here. Come to think of it, though, the climate up here in the mountains is similar to Castroville in California, the self-proclaimed "artichoke capitol of the world.

We pass through small towns with houses painted in bright colors, and hear church bells ringing. Old Toyota Land Cruisers carrying farmers driving to their fields or to town meet or pass us on the rugged roads. The driving habits are a bit more sedate here in the mountains than what we encountered yesterday, thank God. Almost all the villages we pass through have dogs sleeping on the sides of the streets, completely oblivious to cars passing by. At a vista point I take pictures of a boy holding and selling Mucuchíes, a beautiful breed of dog with a black and white face. It is a shepherd breed, and the national dog of Venezuela. There is a well-known painting of Simón Bolívar, the liberator of the country, on a horse with a Mucuchíe that was given to him when he crossed Venezuela. The boy's father seems very disappointed that I don't buy one. I wish I could. Parrots, Mucuchíes—half a pet shop so far.

High up in the Venezuelan portion of the Andes now, Patrick points out a furry-looking plant growing abundantly in the black soil all around us: lamb's ear. I stop to touch it and it is very soft, deserving of its name. Patrick tells me a story about collecting these plants to use for a bed while camping. We're close to the top of the world now; fog, fresh thin air, and billowy white clouds completely surround us. It is so peaceful. A few miles later, there is a giant billboard advertising some sort of progress for Venezuela—this is probably the most remote, and unlikely place for a billboard, it must have been something to get it here and construct it.

Our afternoon destination is Mérida, where we will spend a few days and Patrick will meet up with some friends. Many miles downward, we make a pit stop for *fresas con crema*: fresh strawberries and cream, a country delight. The store also has an assortment of glass bottles in colors ranging from amber to green that glow with the sun shining through them. An "antique" store on the side of the road has an assortment of junk, including a mannequin general sitting in a chair, adorned with a jacket full of medals—what every household needs. At another stop, I refuse to buy a blanket emblazoned with a picture of a tiger on a black background that Patrick tries to talk me into. Utterly hideous would be an understatement. This not-purchased blanket will provide mirth years later.

We arrive in Mérida on a street with yellow blooming trees. On the side of the road underneath these pretty trees sits a Chevy Nova from the early '80s. To call it a piece of junk would be a compliment. It's totally rusted out and the trunk has many holes in it, including holes where the tail lights should be, yet it has a lock and chain holding the trunk closed. Why, oh why? This is the kind of vehicle that still inhabits the roads of Venezuela: beaters from the '70s and '80s just spewing out smog. Since the price of gas is not an issue here, one can see why they still exist. A politically correct Prius owner from California would probably have a heart attack seeing one of these—or at least a fit of self-righteousness.

We drive to an apartment in the middle of town where I meet some of Patrick's friends, who are also Fulbright scholars here in Venezuela; he met them some time back in the city of Maracaibo. They are getting ready to leave and are trying to sell all the stuff in the apartment. Adam makes a *"Remate Total"* (Closeout Sale) sign and tapes it to a mattress outside. He advises an elderly potential customer that each mattress comes with a pretty girl. He definitely has a used-car-salesman smile.

Patrick and I have lunch down the street in a small place owned by a man who claims he is a former airline pilot. On the wall there is a poster of the Argentine soccer team, for some reason. After lunch we want to take the famous aerial tram up to the top of the Andes, but we are told it is shut down because of the weather. I purchase two wooden statues carved and painted in traditional Venezuelan dress, similar to some of the ones I saw at Patrick's hosts' home (one of which I have kept—it's pictured on the cover of this book). My dad had Googled this area before I'd departed for Venezuela and told us about a store we now visit, which sells over 900 flavors of ice cream: the world record. There are flavors such as shrimp, eel, trout, garlic, and ham and cheese, along with the

BREAD + FISH, MÉRIDA VENEZUELA

mundane such as chocolate and vanilla. I don't recall all the flavors we tasted, but shrimp was among them. Not bad—a little weird, but not bad.

After arriving back at the apartment we go out with Adam, Patricia, and Steve for some sandwiches for dinner. I try Maltin, a Venezuelan malt beverage that I am told about. Not hideous, as described by some at the table, but "interesting" as my grandmother used to say. We plan to spend the night outside of town at the mountain home of a friend of Patricia's, in a small array of cottages. We drive there in the Yaris and Patricia's car. The air is cold and the windshield constantly fogs up. After driving in what seems like endless fog we finally arrive at the friend's cottage. After a few beers, a lively geography discussion ensues among the Fulbright scholars. I don't think I can compete with this bunch, and besides, I'm exhausted. I head for the back room with its tiny, creaking bunk beds.

In the morning I meet a bashful Rottweiler outside who is delighted to be fed some scraps. We have pancakes for breakfast and then leave, as I want to go mountain climbing with Patrick, an alternative he has suggested since the tram is out of order. We park near the end of a road that has lots of litter around. It never ceases to amaze and anger me how people can do this to a beautiful landscape. On our ascent we meet a small young calf, which we both pet. What a sweet, lovely creature. We hike for several hours. The air is so fresh up here. The climb is worth it—wonderful views of the Andes. It starts to drizzle, so we decide to head down the mountain. Soaked, we arrive back at our Yaris and have to settle for dirty laundry as replacement for our wet clothes.

Back in Mérida, we walk the streets. I see a beautiful metal sculpture of bread and fishes, one of the symbols of Christianity, on a wooden church door. The stores are closed on Sunday (lovely—as in my native country), but today there is a music festival in the streets, so we listen for a while. Hungry, we stop by a small place and have some smoked trout and rooster soup for lunch. There is a soccer game on TV. The other patrons look at us and wonder where we are from. I'm guessing foreigners are few and far between up here.

On the way back to the apartment I see a pizza place with a Ninja Turtle sign. So there is culture here after all! Their slogan is: *el sabor de los quesos* (the flavor of cheese—and they do like their cheese here in Venezuela). We help Adam and Steve paint the apartment so they can get their deposit back, and have pizza for dinner, but sadly not from the Ninja Turtle place. We then take Steve to the bus station, as he is leaving tonight, and are suddenly surrounded by fires on the streets. The students here in Mérida have taken to the streets to protest the forthcoming closure of RCTV, a public TV station in Caracas that is critical of President Chávez. At issue is the renewal of the radio broadcast license, which Chávez wants to suspend for what he says is the station's role in the 2002 coup that briefly overthrew Venezuela's democratically elected government. Steve decides nonetheless to wait at the bus stop, and we head back. There are traffic jams everywhere, but Adam knows some of the back roads through Mérida, which has a lot of one-way streets. We pass a military checkpoint, where I see a scared young soldier probably not more than 18. The protests and fires have created much anxiety for everyone here. We finally make it past Mérida and arrive back at the cottage and meet some visitors from the U.S. who have come to see Patricia's friend Rebecca. The bashful Rottweiler gets a treat from me, and it's another night of listening to snoring and creaking beds.

It's 6:30 a.m.: rise and shine. We drive to Mérida one more time to say goodbye to Patrick's friends, and Patrick and I head back to Caracas. We take a different route from the one coming here, and the roads over the Andes are even more winding. I stop at a roadside stand where a vendor is selling honey and pollen. The honey is great, the pollen even better. I'm sure my son Christian would be interested in this as well; he introduced me to propolis, a resinous mixture that honeybees collect from tree buds, sap flows, or other botanical sources.

We switch drivers, and Patrick scares the crap out of me with his race driving; the heart rate is now well above normal. I do get him to slow down a bit by telling him we are not from here, we don't have to drive like the other inhabitants.

The flatlands are hot, the complete opposite of the Andes. As we drive north on the freeway I see a bicycle approaching us going

PLANTAIN BUC, VENEZUELA

the wrong way. This really takes the cake—what is wrong with these people? All of a sudden I see an old light blue VW Bug in front of us carrying a bunch of plantains on a roof rack, tailgating a semi, which is pulling three other backwards-facing trucks stacked together like building blocks. I ask Patrick to hold the car steady as I snap several pictures of this spectacle.

We pull over for lunch. Even under the covered roof of the restaurant,

LEMON GRASS

it is hot. We order steak with yucca, and a young Venezuelan woman tries to practice her English with us.

After lunch, we switch drivers again and continue. Another military control point, but the guy in our lane, who has a machine gun, smiles and waves us on. Near the town of San Carlos, we come to a toll road, which, because it is a toll road, is in very good shape. To the right are vast wetlands with what look like mangroves in the distance, glistening in a blue haze in the midday heat—another wonderful photo opportunity. Traffic comes close to a standstill in what appears to be a funeral in the next town, Valencia. Do they have oranges here too?

As dusk approaches, a heavy rainstorm unleashes its full fury on the parched land, hopefully bringing some cooling later. It is now pitch black as we approach the outskirts of Caracas. More about driving habits: in addition to all the aforementioned elements, I now see people running across the freeway, if you can believe that. Drivers are speeding, half the cars have no lights on, or just their brights, and people pass on the left and right. I've seen a lot in my life of driving, but Venezuelans are, simply put, just plain nuts.

We finally arrive in Caracas and opt for a Chinese place near Patrick's hosts' home for dinner. It's strange to me to hear a Chinese waiter speaking in Spanish. We have some good soup and a Polar beer—yes, beer, not bear—to go with it.

After dinner, we go up in the elevator to the penthouse and are a little embarrassed as we step out, sweaty, dirty, and tired from the road, to find a big family dinner going on. We are greeted warmly and are invited to have some lemongrass tea and coffee beans covered with chocolate. That tea was the finest I have ever tasted, and my first lemongrass tea. Patrick's host family has graciously invited me to stay, and after "good nights" we fall into bed exhausted. What a difference from that creaky bunk bed in the mountains.

In the early morning, I hear strange sounds and look out the window to see some vultures on the adjoining rooftops. I roll back over and fall asleep again. I mumble "bye" to Patrick as I hear him leaving later to go to work at the school. I take some vitamins with a glass of water and go back to sleep, finally waking up at 4:00 p.m. It had just been an exhausting trip.

Patrick phones me, and after getting dressed I walk down the hill to meet him. From nearly every second window I hear pots and pans banging, a chorus of kitchen denizens run amok. I meet Patrick and ask him what on earth is going on here, and he tells me this is the way people protest—in the safety of their homes. An interesting but incredibly noisy approach. It again has to do with the impending closure of the RCTV station. We decide to drive around to look for a restaurant for dinner, but the places Patrick knows are closed when we reach them. We finally find an open place and sit down. After some wonderful fresh melon juice we eat a simple meal. At one of the neighboring tables some diners are devouring *arepas* filled with about five pounds of cheese. OK, I exaggerate, but they do have a fondness for cheese here. Baseball is on TV—they also broadcast all U.S. games in which Venezuelan players are playing—and Venezuelans are crazy about the game. Our home team, the San Francisco Giants, has had multiple great players from Venezuela. As we leave the restaurant, I ask the waiter if I may take his picture, and he poses in the classic waiter pose with some bottles on his tray, grinning from ear to ear.

The next morning Patrick wanders into a clinic to get a medical appointment as I order my first *desayuno*, or breakfast, by myself, more by pointing than speaking. Pastries and coffee, not too hard. Patrick is unsuccessful in getting an appointment, so we decide to drive downtown. Our host has invited us to come to the building where he works to see a spectacular collection—not open to the public—of native Venezuelan birds, really a rare treat for us. We are introduced to Dr. Lentino, who graciously shows us some of the fine specimens. There are hummingbirds in their distinctive iridescent colors—not just the "regular" greens and reds, but purples and blues too—and one particularly catches my eye, as the beak is curved, exactly matching the flowers it drinks from. God thought of all things. Dr. Lentino pulls open a drawer full of parrots. It's of

VENEZUELA GREEN PARROT

course a bit sad to see them dead, but at least the birds have been collected and catalogued for future study, which is important if there are endangered species among them. The piece de résistance is an Ecuadorian condor in a box on a shelf that Dr. Lentino proudly displays. Patrick jabs me subtly in the side—take a picture, take a picture!—which I do, cutting off part of the image, unfortunately. We thank Dr. Lentino for his time and go downstairs.

An earsplitting racket greets us as thousands of students and many office workers are marching in the streets to protest the RCTV closure. Industrious vendors sell whistles to further facilitate the noise. As I take pictures, the students pose for me, assuming I'm a foreign reporter. Many are draped in Venezuelan flags and some girls have Venezuelan flags painted on their cheeks. It's peaceful but incredibly

BROWN   PELICAN

loud. After the protesters have passed, we finally manage to get the Yaris out of the garage to return it. The paperwork at the car rental place seems endless, especially because of the dent. After much talk and negotiating on Patrick's side, we are finally able to leave. No luck on getting a policeman bribe reimbursement, though. We stop in a mall for a very late lunch as afternoon rains come down. I also see a very unique high-rise apartment building: the windows poke out a few feet, making the building look like a giant Lego block. A dubious taxi, one without the official yellow license plate, takes us to Patrick's apartment.

Very early start this morning—5:30 a.m. A car service picks us up to take us to the airport. Our driver's mode of communication seems to be grunting, and sparsely at that. Along the road to the airport, vendors are hawking coffee and newspapers. We make our way past the riffraff currency exchangers and other shady types. Breakfast consists of a greasy *arepa*. After a while our flight is announced, and we walk out on the tarmac to an old propeller plane that will take us to Los Roques, where I have booked a three-day package for us. The plane is small and cramped—modern aviation in the U.S. has spoiled us. As some fans turn on, fog comes out of them but doesn't cool much. Sure looks cool though. An adventure back in time.

The plane lands, after a semi-smooth approach, and we walk out the door. My mouth literally drops open as I am dumbstruck by this incredible beauty. Diving pelicans are piercing the aqua-azure ocean as a slight breeze blows over the equatorial, sun-soaked islands. One of our guides for the duration of our stay greets us. It surprises me that Gabriel speaks German—in fact, even better than English. Apparently there is German tourism here. We claim our luggage, which was brought from the plane to the main lobby, and after getting our keys, find our posada, a colorful little abode set among multiple duplicates arranged in somewhat rectangular fashion.

We grab our swim trunks, snorkels, suntan lotion, and cameras and head for one of the three catamarans gently swaying in the breeze on the sea. The sand is a beautiful white. Pelicans continue their diving efforts for the many small fish in the ocean. We take off in the catamaran and have fish for lunch on board along with about ten other people. After sailing past some small islands, we dock near a larger island with a lagoon to go snorkeling. Gabriel calls Patrick a *delfin* when he sees him swim. The lagoon has beautiful coral and numerous small- to medium-sized fish. The water is crystal clear.

I take some fish pictures with a small camera that has a housing for underwater photography, hoping the pictures will turn out. Paying attention to the fish, I forget about my snorkel and accidentally swallow a bunch of salt water. That, the oily fish for lunch, plus the heat and the tide rocking me back and forth in the lagoon, combine to make me seasick and sick to my stomach. Gabriel swims over and helps me to get to shore, where I return my lunch to the beach for the pelicans to fight over. Man, I have never felt so sick in my life.

On board the catamaran again, I drink lots of Coke and water, feeling dehydrated. Back on the island Patrick takes me to the local doctor and she gives me some pills and rehydration fluid. We head to our posada, shower, and rinse our masks and snorkels. Patrick grabs some dinner, and we spend the evening in the posada playing cards after I feel a bit better. The warm trade winds blow gently over us. Every once in a while there is a "ping" on the roof. I finally figure out that some of the sea grape plants that grow next to the posadas are dropping their fruit on the roof. The gentle wind never seems to subside.

After breakfast the next morning, which is a communal affair for the residents of the posadas, we head to the catamarans again, watching our friends the *pelicanos*. Johanna is our tour guide today. She is a delightful girl from Caracas who looks a bit like a chipmunk; she also speaks German and is very happy with her job. We sail to a different island today, where the guides set up a free-standing roof tent for shade. Most of my compatriots are off snorkeling; I opt to sit in a beach chair listening to my iPod. I gaze mesmerized at the turquoise ocean as the wind lulls me to sleep. What a place; it's just beautiful here. After a few hours the catamarans take us to another island—I would have been content to stay here.

Patrick and I decide to take a walk on the next island, which is known for its lobsters. We walk past some ramshackle huts and spy something very amusing: somebody took the head of a lobster and stuck it on the end of a stick, which now pokes out of the ground. We ponder the symbolism of Mr. Lobster-on-a-Stick and continue walking further along the shore as the waves lap at our feet ever so gently. This area has an incredible abundance of small coral and I collect a few treasures to bring home. Back on the island, we have dinner before we return to our posada to play some more gin rummy before falling asleep.

The sound of a propeller airplane is our wakeup call—new visitors arriving. After breakfast our catamarans take us—this time under full sail, with a Venezuelan flag of red, yellow and blue with yellow stars flapping in the wind at the stern—to Kangaroo Island, another island of Los Roques. The guides set up umbrellas and we spend the day swimming, snorkeling, and exploring. We have lunch on the boat and return to the island. I see a dog that has wandered near us from who-knows-where and give him some ice water, which is gratefully lapped up. There are some gray clouds in the sky today, and Gabriel tells me it might rain, which would make today one of the very few days a year that it does rain here. The clouds remain just clouds, though, keeping their moisture.

On the way back we see some flying fish! Spectacular, when you see something in real life that you have only watched on nature pro-grams. The wind blows the baseball cap off my head, and I suppose some shark is wearing it now, showing off to his buddies—look what the careless tourist lost. After landing, Patrick and I decide to climb up the only mountain on our island. Walking toward it, I see children pulling a cart and running on the road and I jump onto the road and frame the image to get one of the best photos I have ever taken, my "Cartier-Bresson" decisive moment. We admire the quartz rock formations as we climb the mountain. Patrick decides to pursue one of his favorite pastimes, stacking rocks, something he is rather adept at and has done in numerous locations to which he has traveled. We leave the finished rock tower, and as the sun goes down we walk past the fishing boats floating on the water and find one of the small bars that is open. Our waiter brings us mojitos, a Cuban drink, and we sip them while lounging in beanbag chairs on the beach, toes in the sand, watching the silver full moon and twinkling stars come out behind the silhouettes of swaying palm trees. Pretty close to heaven, if you ask me.

After some fresh OJ for *desayuno* we embark on our last catamaran outing. I'm sunburned, and one of the other travelers on the boat jokes that I must be a Chávista, or follower of Chávez (they usually wear red shirts). We are on the "lobster" island again, but our lobster head is gone! We return to the boats after another stroll through the shallow lapping waves. On the beach there are some fashion photographers, and Patrick goes over and hams it up with some of the models who are posing for swimsuit ads. Boys will be boys. Our catamaran returns to the island and we reluctantly pack up for our afternoon departure from Los Roques. I give Johanna a goodbye kiss on the cheek. She was such a delightful girl and friendly guide. Farewell, chipmunk.

The old, faithful propeller plane takes us back in an uneventful flight to Caracas, the fans emitting fog once again. As we have time now,

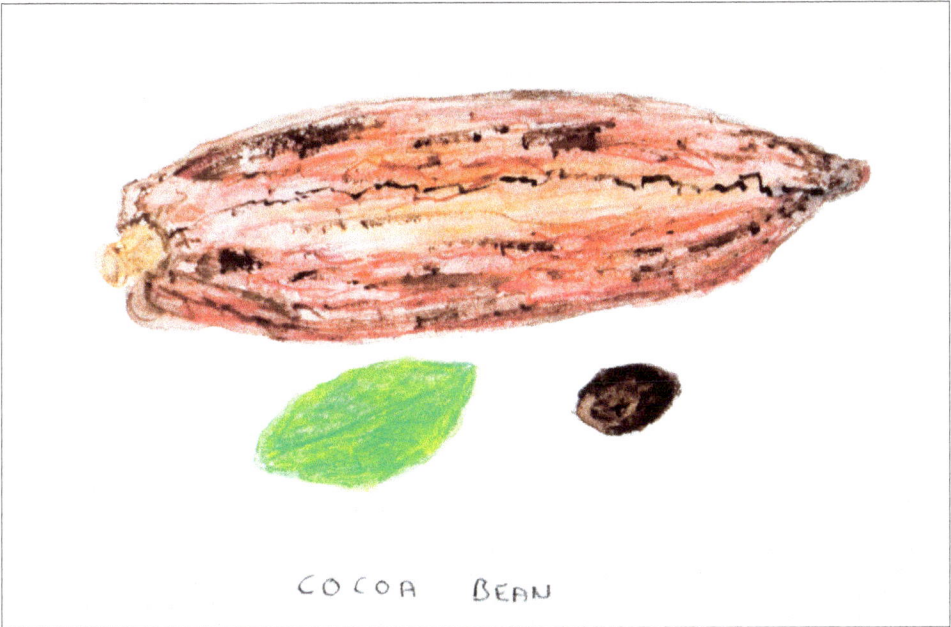

COCOA BEAN

we opt to take the bus back to the city from the airport—a more economical way, too. The bus travels through many neighborhoods and we get to see more of Caracas than before. We disembark and start to walk around. Patrick shows me a mural he is fond of that is very colorful and depicts Venezuelan life. We stop on the street and I chat a bit with a girl selling hand-made jewelry. She is Venezuelan/Haitian, but has a German name, Ingrid, and speaks English. I buy a red, green, and yellow necklace in the colors of Jamaica from her. We stop again, and Patrick buys a hot tamarind. Spicy! We flag down a taxi to take us to Patrick's restaurant. It is another "unofficial" taxi. You would not believe this heap: the roof liner and door panels are gone, and the driver has fabricated some kind of home-made wooden steering wheel. Exhaust fumes pour into the car through the trunk and back seat; it is nauseating. We have some pizza in the restaurant and head home. This time we take a real cab with a yellow license plate. It must be getting close to the end of the driver's shift—he has taken off his tie and hung it on the mirror. We have some chamomile tea before I pack for tomorrow. I thank Patrick's host for his hospitality and by giving him one of my framed photos for his "museum" and then we go to sleep.

We have cold leftover pizza for breakfast and wait outside for the car service. This time we get a guy in an SUV that is all decked out with three TVs in it and flashing glowing lights—"the works." He is listening to R&B as he greets us and grabs our bags, and off we go. Patrick enjoys the music video that's playing. The driver watching TV while driving? Only in Venezuela. Traffic is light this morning, even at the bridge construction zone. At the airport in Caracas we have some coffee that is way too sweet and Patrick buys some waffles, which he tops with the bananas he was carrying. Another emphatic NO! to the currency exchange riffraff.

I buy some presents for home, including some great *gayaba* (guava) chocolate, a Venezuelan specialty. Venezuela is considered to have the very best chocolate in the world. The Criollo cacao bean, the best of the three kinds of cocoa beans that exist, are native to Venezuela, and are sought after by the world's top luxury chocolatiers. The Amazonian rain forest's humid, warm, sub-tropical climate creates these flavorful and aromatic cacao beans. The harvesting, fermentation, and drying processes add to the unique flavor. Then there is the Forastero bean, which is a disease-resistant bean with a strong bitter, astringent flavor and which accounts for 80–90 percent of worldwide production. They are grown primarily in Côte d'Ivoire. The third type of bean is the Trinitario, a cross between the Forastero and Criollo bean. Most experts agree that Chuao Village, a mountainous village in the hills of northern Venezuela, produces the world's best cacao beans. The Criollo cocoa beans of Chuao are processed by hand techniques passed down for 400 years. I didn't learn about this until later: it certainly would have been worth a visit. You have to access it by boat from the sea, though; there are no direct roads from Caracas.

Sadly, as of this writing, Venezuelan cocoa bean growers are dealing with a multitude of problems due to the country's current state of affairs and economic collapse under the current government.

I love chocolate, but then again, who doesn't? Cocoa is also good for your health, the cacao seed contains theobromine-rich alkaloids that strengthen your heart and promote muscle growth, and consuming raw chocolate stimulates serotonin levels in the brain, alleviating depression—as if one needed a justification!

Patrick gives me a long hug. So long, my boy. See you in a few months. After the flight takes off, the beautiful coastline is visible from the porthole once again. The food service is most wonderful: warm nuts, tomato juice, a mimosa, couscous salad, and a steak, along with a peach tart. We will be flying over Haiti and Cuba en route direct to Miami this time. My eyes close as I ponder the past two weeks' incredible adventure. Thanks be to God for this trip, and the many opportunities to photograph, too.

Ten Minutes or 30 Years?

November 2010

The early bird gets the worm: it will be a long drive as well as a long day today. I'm so happy to be able to finally get out and about a bit again and go on a trip to see my friends in Portland. My new toy to aid in this voyage, a navigation system rented for this trip, advises me to turn left at the end of the driveway. I blatantly ignore it by turning right. Politely it informs me that it is recalculating the route. This happens about five or six more times as I navigate towards a Peet's Coffee store. Inside the store there is already a long line in front of the baristas, a sight which would ordinarily be as welcome as a line at the Postal Service, but I'm on a great road trip, so the mood is splendid! With a cafe au lait in one hand and a cup of ice water in the other, I depart, and this time my navigation system is quite happy as I finally follow directions.

The air is crisp and clear this morning and the view from the upper deck of the Richmond–San Rafael Bridge is gorgeous as the sun hovers over the Bay, which looks like a sheet of glass. Highway 101, with a long construction zone around the Santa Rosa area, is no problem today. Luckily it is still early enough for relatively smooth traffic. The Doobies' (or for my younger audience The Doobie Brothers) song "Ukiah" is playing on the radio—how fitting, as the town lies directly on my route. I pass through a town called Hopland (I hope I recall this correctly, as I forgot to take notes in my notebook). It's a lovely town with a Western look. I almost stop for a second cup of coffee, but am going just a bit too fast. I do need to mind the speed limit, which Ms. Navigation also displays, and Kotuku, my little Honda CR-V, has speed control too, so slow down Mr. Road Trip, then you won't miss the coffee shops. An hour later,

SMALL COAST REDWOOD TREE

heavy fog descends during a pit stop for gas. It's very cold, relatively speaking—probably 10 to 15 degrees colder than the Bay Area. I do pull into a drive-through coffee place a little further up the street to get a second jolt of those coffee beans for the upcoming miles. As I continue north, some already bare gray-green gnarled oak trees surround me on both sides of this mountainous stretch of 101.

Quite a bit further on Ms. Navigation is ignored again—I apologize—as I veer right onto the scenic route of the "Avenue of the Giants," a stretch of majestic coastal redwoods. I stop at an information sign and retrieve a brochure. A towering darkness engulfs me on both sides, as these ancient giants let little sunlight through on foggy days. Americans are usually rather proper about their sanitary regulations, but today I opt for the French way, as there are no toilets in sight. I'm sure Mr. Redwood—a specimen chosen slightly away from the roadside and who is most likely more than half a dozen centuries old, judging by circumference—will forgive the peepee in his proximity, a splatter in time, if you'll forgive the nonchalant expression and behavior. There are almost no cars on this isolated route—well, it is November. The aromatic smell of the redwoods fills the inside of the car as I roll down the windows and leave them down for a bit. A few spots where the sun comes through it is warm; otherwise it is cool and damp. Time stands still in such a place.

Many miles later, back on the regular Route 101, I pass through Eureka. The freeway here becomes a long one-way winding stretch directly through town. Having driven through Eureka before in a rainstorm, I cherish today's better weather despite the fog. From glimpses I get left and right, Eureka is a historic city, with Victorian houses and a lumber tradition. A little outside of town, it is time for a very late lunch consisting of some sliced chicken and rosemary potatoes—leftovers from last night. I would have much preferred a glass of wine to the can of root beer that accompanies lunch, but obviously not doable as I'm still driving. As it is rather windy now in addition to the increasing fog, the lunch stop is brief.

Coming into Crescent City, which I saw only through sheets of rain the last time, I stop to photograph some of the maritime sights. I'm surprised to see the occasional bicycle along the freeway, as I thought this was illegal in California. Perhaps not in remote areas.

"Now entering Oregon," the large highway sign on the side of the road proclaims. Uncharted territory! On the last trip up the coast, after driving through both aforementioned cities, I veered off on Highway 199 towards I-5, so the Oregon Coast is something new. As twilight now approaches, the town of Brookings comes into view. Checking in at the motel I lumber, if you'll pardon the Oregonian pun, up to the third-floor room and unpack. Road weariness settles in, but I head downstairs to walk along the rock-and-driftwood beach that I saw from the window above. The smells of salt and the sea are heaven to the senses. It's surprisingly warm, and I later find out that this section of coast is in the "Banana Belt." The motel brochure, as well as some signs outside, declare that this area is a Tsunami Zone—one hopes without any real consequences tonight.

Back in the room, I get my swim trunks and head for the outside heated spa and pool. All the driving exhaustion seems to simply disappear among the whirling rising bubbles. Earlier the receptionist recommended the restaurant adjacent to the motel, and a few sparse lamps light the way through the darkness and fog as I heed her suggestion. It's a rustic place with a nautical theme. A cheerful bubbly waitress greets me, and I order the halibut after a short study of the menu. She asks me if I would like fresh bread and I happily agree. I ask if there is a newspaper lying around, and she manages to scrounge one up for me, telling me that this is the local paper published twice a week. Thank you. The big front-page news is the sinkhole in town caused by rain, and I'm sure that will be the subject of discussion for quite some time to come. The fish arrives. The baked potato is filled to the brim with countless calories and topped with bacon bits. This is no lean cuisine, but oh so good. I chuckle to myself as I receive the "fresh bread," which consists of warmed-up dinner rolls. Oh well, shut up and eat, Mr. Spoiled-by-Food-in-the-Bay-Area. A glass of wine induces sleepiness on the way back to the room. I stop by the reception one more time and ask for a 7 a.m. wake-up call. Oh, what a nice, soft bed. In the middle of the night I wake up one time to the sound of the waves outside the window, unfamiliar sounds to my ear. Can one shut those off, please?

Dawn and the alarm bring morning. I head down for the hot tub and pool again. That is the one thing I always look for first when traveling: a pool and hot tub, if at all possible. I once won a bet as a teenager for a case of beer from my dad by swimming a mile in a pool—I doubt I could do the mile now. Steam rises up from the hot tub in the crisp morning air. A father and his young daughter are the only other occupants. We chat a bit, and it turns out we are practically neighbors, as he is from Morgan Hill, but he says he grew up here. Refreshed, I pack up, check out, and walk to Kotuku, who is still sleeping. In the parking lot some guy is yakking at the top of his voice on his cell phone about MJ-90s, whatever those might be. Pathetic, conducting business outside in a quiet motel parking lot by the sea this early in the morning, if you ask me.

Kotuku is thirsty, so I head out for the next gas fill-up. I'm surprised to see a man pumping his own gas, and ask him if Oregon now has self-serve gas now. He replies, "Shhh, my dad works here. Don't tell anybody." From behind a large motorhome the regular attendant emerges and fills my tank. His name is Rochester, and he tells me a story about filling up a vehicle for over $900. If this is not a fish story that makes you truly wonder about miles per gallon! I ponder raising the question about whether Rochester has a brother named Kodak, but decide not to. I ask for a coffee recommendation and he directs me to Dutch Bros., another drive-through coffee place. Among their offerings is a drink menacingly named the Annihilator. A cheerful girl makes a great and hot cafe latte for me—I opt not to choose the Annihilator—and now the day can start.

Outside of town, I see my first logging truck; now I'm sure it's Oregon. The coast is beautiful: dunes, driftwood, rocks, lagoons, the soft sunshine bathing them. I stop in Port Orford, as there is a wonderful view of the sea from there. I say good morning to a man with his bulldog watching the ocean. As we start talking he tells me he is a retired grip man from the San Francisco cable cars. Small world. The adage about a dog and its owner often looking similar seems to be holding true. Both look grizzled by time, but have a laid-back disposition. The dog has a funny name, but I cannot recall it now—I think it was something like Asteroid or Comet. It fit him well. I say goodbye and continue up the beautiful coast.

In Coos Bay, another big lumber town, I stop to run Kotuku through a car wash—he needs it. Afterwards, parked near the bay, I watch from a pier along with several other spectators as a procession of logging trucks moves close to a large freighter from Panama moored at the dock, and then get their loads lifted by a giant crane onto the ship. It is a fascinating spectacle. Rather reluctantly I depart from this full-scale version of playing with toy cars, or

ON THE OREGON COAST

lumber and cranes, as the case may be.

It turns out the car wash was a waste of time and money, as it starts to sprinkle and then rain lightly. The result is intensified by the trucks in front of me whirling up water with gusto. The coastal scenery varies from rocky beaches to high cliffs. At a stopover point near some high cliffs, my curiosity is piqued when I see some people intently gazing over the edge. Monkey see, monkey do, and I spy dozens of sea lions perched on a huge rock hundreds of feet below as the thundering surf breaks all around them. It seems peculiar that they should choose a spot like this. Perhaps a safe place from predators, but it must be an enormous effort to get onto the rocks.

It is now just overcast as I enter Newport, traveling over a very high steel bridge that affords a view of a fishing fleet and a picturesque town. This must be a bustling summer vacation spot. Even now, in November, there are plenty of signs of tourism—stores displaying their welcome signs outside, and parking lots full with out-of-state license plates—many of course from California and Washington. Ms. Navigation tells me to continue north on 101 and I obey, as it is already late afternoon with plenty of miles to go. I have always liked those big orange and red Tillamook cheddar cheese blocks, and I envision them marching in rows to their destinations in supermarkets as the City of Tillamook appears on the screen. All of a sudden a stench of cow dung fills the air and my thoughts quickly turn to rapid departure and fresh air. What a rude awakening from dreams of marching cheese. Luckily, not too much later a long, winding, two-lane highway helps me flee this stench. The birch trees on both sides of the road are bare, their leaves a muddled mushy goo. A cold, icy river rushes alongside past boulders, and the dark shadows of the valley engulf Kotuku, as commuters and trucks—all with their lights on—now appear sporadically, coming from the opposite direction, at high speeds. As I turn onto Highway 26 as directed by Ms. Navigation, I am surprised that she switches to night mode, a pleasant surprise and less distracting to driving. A low fog hangs over the now-flat valley as the last hint of light dips below the horizon and the moon smiles. Evening commute traffic is fairly heavy, and I'm happy I'm being directed by Ms. Navigation. A few more turns and then I arrive in Beaverton at my oldest friends' house. Hey, Big Patrick and Sanae!

My son Patrick's girlfriend, Hannah, who is house-sitting for her sister in Portland, is going to show me Tacoma today, as I make my first venture into Washington State on this trip. After the obligatory coffee fill-up, Ms. Navigation sends me over the Ross Island Bridge to pick up Hannah. The fall colors on the trees are a palette of yellows, reds, and oranges of every shade imaginable. I ring the bell and Doogan, Hannah's sister's dog, greets me alongside Hannah. Hug from Hannah, tail-wagging from Doogan, a very friendly fellow. I'm hoping for some halfway decent weather, but it's drizzly and gray. Hannah shows me some tricks on the navigation system, as she will be the navigator today, and the navigation system is ignored once more, as Hannah knows a short-cut to the freeway. I hope she is not sulking—Ms. Navigation, that is.

Once across the Columbia River Bridge on I-5, Washington State welcomes us. I always liked that, rather than "now entering"—it is so much more friendly. Hannah and I chit-chat about the Bay Area, and my son Patrick's trip and intended six-month stay in Senegal in West Africa with a stopover in Germany to see family. He is so adventurous.

About an hour into the trip to Tacoma, I see a very small patch of blue sky through the mass of gray above. Hannah informs me that that's what is known as a "sucker hole," or false promise of good weather. Much to my chagrin, she turns out to be quite correct. The clouds thicken more and more as we approach Tacoma.

We are both hungry, and Hannah suggests various alternatives, among them the "best" chicken she has ever eaten. That sounds like a winner to me, and we steer towards Southern Chicken. I am amused that we are having southern food near Puget Sound, not seafood. But was she ever right: fried chicken, the best yams I have ever tasted, corn bread, mashed potatoes, and hot coffee—what a feast! The friendly waitress sits briefly at our table and gives Hannah the yam recipe. The place is packed. We can't finish it all, and take

YAMS - SOUTHERN KITCHEN

our doggie bags with us. Fat chance, Doogan—I'm eating this. I talk with the chef/cashier and he asks me if I want to order a pie for Thanksgiving. I politely decline and tell him that I live in California. That's not a problem, he tells me, and says he has shipped via Fed-Ex to the East Coast and to a lieutenant in Afghanistan via a military transport plane. That's long-distance chicken indeed, although I wonder whether it's a proper use of government transportation. Perhaps there was some extra space aboard. I'm planning to save the yams for Big Patrick as he is from Mississippi, and I'll bet he can appreciate great yams. This was one of Hannah's hang-outs in college and I can see why.

Amid thickening fog, we drive to UPS—a name that never ceases to amuse me. No, it's not the package carrier, although I should give them equal billing as I mentioned their competitor above—it stands for University of Puget Sound. The streets here are wide and all the houses have huge yards in front, mostly lawns, but with many trees, as well. It's an unfamiliar sight to a Bay Area resident to see so much open space. After parking at the university, we start to walk on the campus. There is some sports activity going on despite it being Sunday. The trees are showing off again. Hannah shows me a mysterious place in front of a building where, if you stand at just the right spot, you can hear an echo, a small phenomenon that works! Inside one of the buildings there are some blown glass pieces by Dale Chihuly, who attended school here. The style is easily recognizable. Bright yellow ginkgo trees surround a glass atrium/cafeteria outside. I'm sure Hannah is looking forward to showing Patrick all this.

As we leave, Hannah tells me that there is a park at the end of the city right next to Puget Sound that she wants to show me. Driving, we are engulfed by fog and clouds and Hannah says, "The Puget Sound is there, I promise." A fishing boat and a ferry boat are dim silhouettes in the gray fog over gray sea. We park the car and climb up a slope, and Hannah shows me a tree she planted at a wedding. Gravity makes for an easy, if somewhat slippery, descent. After getting back in the car, we continue along the foggy sea as I hear more promises of the Puget Sound actually being there, and then into downtown, where we park across from the Glass Museum. Hannah poses for a photograph with a metal sculpture of a traveler with a suitcase in front of a railway station, a sculpture that depicts the pioneer days. Walking across a bridge over the freeway, we see numerous incredible glass works. Hannah tells me that on sunny days, it is just a bright spectacular burst of color from down below. Past some fountains, we stop at the museum's gift shop and at a gallery. It is a bit too late, though, to visit the museum. In the shop, we see a book of drawings created by children that were then turned into glass art by professional glass blowers. Remarkable, and I'm sure a thrill for the kids to see their visions turned three-dimensional. Inside the gallery I see a glass sculpture of what looks like an aluminum trailer. I take a picture for Patrick, as he has just bought one this spring that he found in Big Sur, which now resides in a storage lot. A bit tired now (at least I am), we have a cup of tea. I find a specialty cupcake shop and encourage four of its denizens to accompany me in a box. Three make it home. I will leave you to guess who ate the fourth one. It's time to go, and I'm grateful that Hannah is driving back tonight so I can nap and stretch a bit. Rain follows us all the way home. Doogan is very happy to see us back. Thank you for the trip, Hannah. And now, to Beaverton, Ms. Navigation, if you please.

It's really nice to have full service at the gas stations in Oregon. The attendant even cleans my front and back windshields as I get gas the next morning. Astounding! He recommends a small shop across the street for coffee, and good coffee it is, along with a puff pastry that wants to accompany it. I'm one of two people in the place this early, and the girl behind the counter is very attentive and friendly, getting that coffee just right.

It is the second time in a few days driving over the bridge on I-5 into Washington State, this time with the destination of Port Angeles. It's overcast, but with much better visibility than the trip to Tacoma. The drive is uneventful, however, this time without any "sucker holes." Ms. Navigation steers me left of Olympia, the capitol of Washington State, and then up Highway 101 along the Hood Canal, Dabob, and then Quilcene Bay. White caps dot the sea and the wind manifests itself in the groaning, bending trees. There are several closed fireworks stands on the side of the road;

some of them proclaim to be illegal, a rather strange and blatant advertisement prone to attract the attention of the local police, one tends to think.

It's been too many hours on the road again—Ms. Navigation would be more of an asset were she to suggest periodic pit stops to deter such long drives as this, but perhaps she is just being polite. Out of the corner of my eye I spy another drive-through coffee place on the right, just before passing it (training acquired from years of peripheral vision use while driving taxi) and still manage to pull in. I order a first for me: a crème brûlée coffee, which is quite tasty, I might add.

The road bends inland now for a bit before it borders the water at Sequim Bay again. As I drive past an Indian casino, Port Angeles comes into view below. Despite the many miles on the road, I want to see at least part of Olympic National Park before it gets dark. I should stop at the Visitor Information Center first but don't, and Ms. "Now-Go-Straight" sends me up Hurricane Ridge Road into the park. I arrive at a ranger station where a sign proclaims that the road is closed ahead. Never having taken signage all that seriously, I proceed anyway. There are pine cones and small branches scattered and strewn all over the road. There must have been one heck of a storm here last night, and as the road comes to a dead end and a closed gate I see snow-capped mountain peaks in the distance. So close but yet so far. I take a few pictures and while doing so drop my glasses, which I just replaced two weeks ago because they were scratched up. I'm none too happy with my clumsiness. I turn around and Ms. Know-It-All brings me back to the Visitor Center. All right, all right, sorry; I'm taking my scratched glasses out on her. The ranger inside confirms that the storm passed last night, and suggests an alternative that might still be reached in daylight: Lake Mills, an artificial lake with a dam at the end of it that he says will be the first dam to be torn down next year to restore the salmon habitat. There is hope for humanity, it seems.

Past a raging river, the conifers crowd and encroach ever closer. Lichen, moss, and ferns form the undergrowth. There are no other cars. Finally the lake appears. It seems to be man-made on one end. An icy wind howls over it, and majestic snow-capped mountains rise in the distance. Following the trees along the side, I hope for an aerial view of the lake, and many curves later it is fulfilled. I now must confess to the blatant kidnapping of a small lush green conifer about a foot tall on the side of the road. I half expect Smokey the Bear to jump out to foil this attempt, but perhaps he is hibernating already. This little conifer will have quite a story to tell the redwood tree at my house and vice versa.

I must jump ahead for a brief moment at this point, and confess that on my return trip later to California, which I won't write about as it was a boring and exhausting marathon drive down I-5 (with the exception of a snowstorm at the Oregon/California border), I swallowed hard a few times at the agricultural inspection point. The conifer now resides in my loft next to the redwood tree along with—well, we will come to that part later.

Rain starts to fall as I make my way down the mountain road and back to Port Angeles, on the Strait of Juan de Fuca, where my hotel is. As I approach in navigation night mode again, logging trucks pass me on the other side at their usual breakneck speeds. I always try to stay as far to the right as possible in such situations, as one wouldn't stand a chance in a collision. A lumber mill is lit up with

TAKE HOME FISH CO.

bright lights, and a gigantic freighter from Alaska sits at the port waiting to have its belly filled with logs. An intriguing sight, but I just want to check in at the hotel now. The main road has two one-way lanes going through town, as in so many other towns in Washington and Oregon. Sparkling white Christmas lights hugging the silhouettes of tree branches add a warm, welcoming glow to the town.

"Arriving at destination," I am informed, and I park Kotuku kitty-corner from the hotel. After bringing my bags upstairs, I pick up the phone, as a sign at the empty reception desk advises me to do. A clerk appears from down the hall, and I check in. I am one of only two guests in this off season. I inquire about the place I parked out-side, and am informed that the one and only meter maid in town is sick, so not to worry, but that they do have a lot on the side street too, if I am so inclined to park there. I am amused, and wish the meter maid a speedy recovery, sort of.

After I freshen up in one of the washrooms, which are shared in the hall, Kotuku and Ms. Navigation steer me towards dinner. I really should give her a name, perhaps Never Fail or Know It All? Perhaps not, as for the first time she is off by about 200 feet from the correct address of the restaurant. Perhaps she is fatigued from the trip, too. The reader will undoubtedly now wish to formulate an opinion on my poor choice of ordering a steak near the sea, but I had fish two nights in a row and I'm rather hungry. The order of fresh chanterelles on the side seals the deal. The stomach was a bit smaller than the eyes, however, so the to-go box will serve as lunch or dinner for tomorrow. My room is very quiet, except for the occasional rattling of the heater and the pitter-patter of raindrops on the window, as slumber sets in.

The phone was set to ring, but dawn and the pitter-patter on the windows wake me up before that. After a quick shower, it's downstairs, as I plan to drive to the most northwestern point in the lower US today, Cape Flattery, no matter the weather. Right next to the hotel there is a diner, but I opt for Cock-a-Doodle doughnuts on the other side as I want to get going. Six assorted donuts—nothing like a nutritionally balanced healthy breakfast. As I grab the donuts, my camera, the coffee, and my keys, the latter fall to the floor. One woman picks them up for me and another opens the front door. Boy, people in the countryside sure are nice. Turning on the wipers and the radio, I hear about arguments between the Ottawa senators (the real ones, not the hockey team). Then it sinks in: it's a Canadian radio station, as Port Angeles is directly across the border from Victoria.

The rain is getting heavier and heavier as I travel west. Several logging trucks come barreling down the narrow road, their head-lights flashing maliciously. I say a little prayer for some clearing skies so I can take some pictures. Suddenly a deer runs across the road, but I manage to avoid it, as does the car behind me. The dark clouds above the Strait of Juan de Fuca look ominous, and it seems like nighttime at 9:00 in the morning. Waves crash onto the shore that edges on the two-lane highway, and the whitecaps are whipped to a frenzy by the ice-cold wind. Oddly enough, Ms. Navigation is in day mode despite the dreary dark skies. Mile after mile of sea and storm, then trees for a bit and back to the rugged coastline. Entering Neah Bay, the clouds lift and the rain stops; my prayer has been answered. I stop at the Makah Indian Reservation Museum and buy a permit for the trail that I want to visit, departing quickly so as to not miss this God-given break in the weather. Winding through the few streets of Neah Bay, I see fishing boats, low houses, and trailers.

Another few miles and I come to the end of the road. I am the only car and/or person here. What fool besides yours truly would venture out in this inclement weather? Both cameras slung over my shoulder, I walk through a wet and chilly cedar forest. The earthen trail is interspersed with wooden walkways. Puddles left and right—the trees drip rain when the wind hits them. I should have brought my heavy coat; I'm freezing in my vest, and I'm normally warm-blooded. After about 45 minutes I am rewarded with a view of the Pacific. Rugged cliffs rise out of the stormy sea and the waves wash over a rock that looks like an enormous whale. Suddenly a rainbow appears over the ocean, God's promise to us to never flood the earth again. It is beautiful. I am frozen stiff now and make my way back on the trail. Close to the empty parking lot, a very small cedar tree jumps up, hides underneath my vest, and begs a ride to California, to

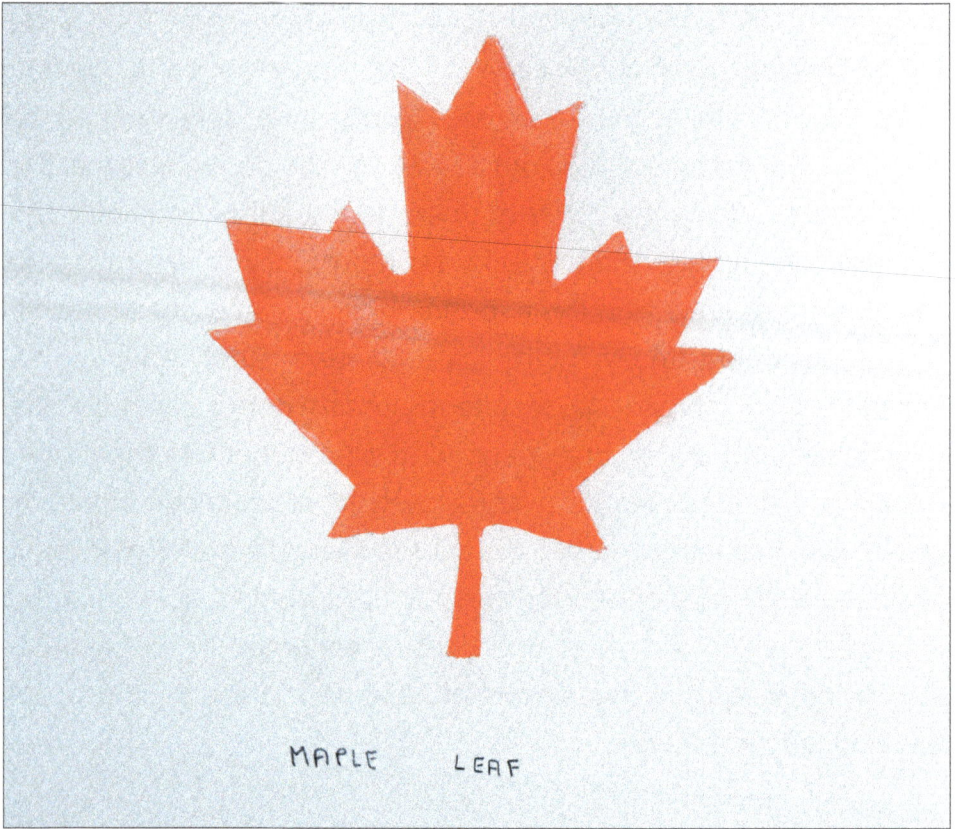

MAPLE   LEAF

reside and perhaps converse with my redwood and the recently abducted conifer. With a bit of soil that just happened to follow us too, my little cedar now inhabits an empty coffee cup.

The heater is cranked up and the senses are slowly restored. To the south, a few beaches with driftwood and rocks lead the way to a fish hatchery. In front of it sits a rusty metal salmon sculpture surrounded by round flat rocks. I only meet one hatchery worker, and after a short exchange I walk downstairs to look at the outside basins, but the water is too dark to see the fish. It's still cold and getting colder by the minute and I decide to drive back to Neah Bay, where a place that sold smoked salmon caught my eye. Parking Kotuku, I enter the small shed where a man is attending to his smoker. It smells delicious in here. He lifts a metal tray out from the smoker, releasing the aroma of alder wood, and rearranges the fish on different layers, as well as removing some of it. Appropriately, he wears a sweatshirt with a fish printed on it. We chat for a bit, and he gives me a sample of the fish he has just smoked. It just melts in your mouth, and the flavor is astounding. He tells me a funny story of how some lady came to his store and remarked, "Oh that looks easy, you just take some wood and smoke the fish. Probably takes 10 minutes." I would imagine this man has perfected his trade over 30 years, in addition to his fishing skills. I purchase one order of fresh smoked steelhead trout and two vacuum-packed ones from the Take Home Fish Co.—one for my friends in Portland and one for my cat Calvin's caretakers, Bill and Nancy.

On the return route, I will travel through Olympic National Park again. Not five minutes after I start to drive, the heavens open up again and another deluge of rain falls from the gray skies. Logging trucks—what else—their lights shining bright, pass me on the other side again as I approach Lake Crescent. The mountains surrounding this slate gray to light green lake are covered with snow down to the lower elevations, and are dotted with pine trees aching under their heavy white load. It's a quiet sort of beauty of late fall, early winter. Dark leafless branches hang over parts of the dormant lake, dreaming of spring. It is a contemplative drive back.

This time I arrive in Port Angeles at dusk. A short visit to my hotel room where I eat my dinner in a box from last night, which I manage to heat in a microwave I find in a room that was left open down the hall, and then it's out once more under partly cloudy skies (as the weather people on TV like to say) to walk through the town a bit. Near the terminal for the ferries to Victoria, which is closed for the night, there is a large wooden building housing art galleries and a restaurant. Along the side children have decorated a fence with colorful cut-out drawings of fish. It's such a cheerful sight in the cold of evening. A few very late rays of light barely peek through the clouds. Wandering some side streets, I see a sign gracing the sidewalk that advises that "snow shoes are on sale," a purchase I do not wish to experience. Tired now, I buy a piece of boysenberry pie with vanilla ice cream from the diner for dessert, pick up a Seattle paper from the newspaper box outside, and trudge up the stairs to my room. It's been an eventful, long day.

With a 7 a.m. check-out, I forget my key in the room. Oh well, don't want to wake the desk clerk. I guess the maid will find it. After yesterday's overdose of donuts, and so as not to deprive the local police of nourishment, I settle for just a bear claw and coffee this time. The Christmas lights on the trees still twinkle as I leave town. A French chanson plays on the radio, and I am reminded once again that Canada is close by. It is followed by Mozart's Eine Kleine Nachtmusik, and then some French hip-hop music. It's the most unusual combination of music I have ever heard on a radio station. Dawn rises over the Strait of Juan de Fuca. It is bitter cold. I see an "Elk X-ing" sign on the right side of the road, but it turns out to be false advertising. The radio plays a French chanson-type version of "Hotel California," which sounds bizarre, followed by more classical music. Amusing, eh? My destination this morning before I head back to Beaverton is Port Townsend, a recommendation from Hannah.

Shortly before arriving, I smell the stench of a paper mill, which is nauseating, to put it mildly. Before pulling into Port Townsend, I stop by the Visitor Information Center. It is staffed by two delightful gentlemen, one of whom has been there since the 1960s, and the other an immigrant from England. We chat for a while, and I am informed about uptown and downtown and much more, as well as given a good breakfast recommendation. This is a real port and shipyard, not a Fisherman's Wharf–type tourist attraction. I park near another ferry terminal and walk into a restaurant overlooking Port Townsend Bay. It's early and quiet with only a few customers. The waitress brings me a menu and after perusing it I ask her for a recommendation, as I can't decide between the corned beef hash or eggs Benedict. She recommends the latter, and I am not disappointed. A guy walks in and sits at the counter; he is wearing flip-flops and shorts. He must be nuts; the attire for most of the other occupants is down jackets. To each his own, I guess. Properly nourished, I drive and park downtown.

Port Townsend is a historic town with beautiful intricate Victorian architecture, which I would not have expected up here. It is getting colder by the minute as the icy wind comes in off the bay. I duck into an art gallery that has some beautiful Northwest Coastal Tribes artwork. I particularly like a lithograph card I purchase with an image that has not just the traditional black, red, and white motif but also other colors in it — a break with tradition and a fine example of creative thinking. A mailman enters the shop and looks glad to do so, reminding one of the old adage: neither rain nor...well, you know the rest. Despite my interest in the novelty of the old Victorian houses, the unique art galleries, and the abundant nautical scenery, I still duck into a shop every 50 feet because the wind is so bitterly cold. I can't imagine how cold this town must be in the deep of winter. Now for uptown: the smell of a bakery draws me inside, and I buy a loaf of sourdough bread for my friends, since it's hard to find in Portland. The bakery has a reprint of a magazine article in the window: "As recommended by Sunset Magazine." It's hard to leave the smell of bread. Next on the agenda, kitty-corner, is a century-old grocery store that features fine local specialties: alder-wood smoked salmon, Washington State wines, apple butter, and boysenberry soda—what fun. The homeward stretch beckons, and heater on once again, Kotuku steers southbound aided by Ms. Navigation. Leaving town there is a roundabout—I personally love to drive in them. It reminds me of the ones in France, and then again the ones that were built in the People's Republic of Berkeley, although some of the latter have stop signs at the entrance that defeat the purpose, if you can believe such bureaucratic stupidity, probably authorized in triplicate. More than once I have ignored those stop signs; catch me if you can.

On the road to the Hood Canal, I spy a herd of swine. Their thick skin—dare I say chicharrón—apparently protects them quite well from this wind. The bridge across the Hood Canal has flashing high wind warnings. Fortunately, Highways 3 and 16 are pleasant and multi-lane and move right along, as I am now road-weary. At Gig Harbor, before the toll bridge, I consume lunch in the form of a DQ chocolate sundae with peanuts—so as not to deprive you, dear reader, of further ramblings about food. Thus strengthened, Kotuku and I once again brave the high winds. We merge onto I-5 and pass Tacoma. It is now heavy afternoon rush-hour traffic, and the rain makes driving unpleasant. Last stop: Olympia, where I pull off over the stern objections of Ms. Navigation to find a drive-through coffee store. It's OK, sweetheart, we will go back to I-5 in just a wee bit. I ask for a café au lait and, receiving a quizzical look, correct myself: latte. I explain the French term, and the girl says, "My grandmother is French, I really should go back to school and learn that language." Rain, rain, and more rain all down I-5 through

Washington and Oregon. Portland traffic has become quite bad over the last decade—must be all those Californians with their bad driving habits who moved up north. I chuckle as I think of the joking automotive warning Big Patrick gave me before I departed: if you see an old Asian man with Washington license plates driving a big Buick, beware and pull to the side as quickly as you can. He must have been parked that day. Exhausted, I arrive in Beaverton, where Big Patrick greets me at the door: "Welcome home!"

The Goldpanner at Maxwell
January 2011

The forecast the night before was for low ground fog with minimum visibility in the Central Valley and the Bay Area. As usual the TV weatherman droned on and on endlessly about it. I can take a hint, and thus won't bore you with my morning coffee stories, as I have in past stories—just sip it, and be quiet—after all you don't want a comparison with the TV weatherman, do you Mr. Author?

I'm on my way to Redding, CA, for a night, as one of my photos was accepted for an exhibit at the Turtle Bay Exploration Park Museum and Gallery, which I was very excited about. The image is of a frozen mountain lake with a dried tree lying in it.

Highway I-80 is very congested today, probably because of the aforementioned fog. Next to me is a semi, one of the muddiest and dirtiest I have ever seen. He has a broom attached to the rig, although it doesn't seem to have been put to very good use here. Perhaps just a decoration or conversation piece. As I pass him, the Carquinez Bridge appears. Normally you can see far below this massive, high bridge, but not today; the TV weatherman must be gloating. More miles eastward, I see a funny sight: three crows on one telephone pole, separated from each other just enough for comfort—better if you are not a morning crow, I think. I hope they don't run into any customers from a store I see on the right called "Guns, Fishin' + Other Stuff." Only in America, I think to myself. One of my favorite sights comes up on the left, the cow jumping over the moon sign; that always makes me smile.

SACRAMENTO MARSHLANDS

The fog is very clammy and just refuses to lift. Wait a minute—Davis? Did I miss my turn-off looking at the scenery? Never saw a Davis sign before. Sure did, missed it. I'm way past the 505, almost in Sacramento. Oh well, it will be a detour then. I have only been in Sacramento a few times in spring and summer, and the view of the Sacramento River has always been wonderful. Today, gray glimpses from high up on the freeway overpass appear only sporadically, along with looming silhouettes of dark oak trees, sticking out their branches in winter resignation. They follow me onto I-5, dipping back into their blankets of fog here and there. You can tell you are in the country when you see a sign that says "Dirt for Sale."

Somewhere near the town of Maxwell I pull over at the rest stop to stretch and—well, you-know-what road trip necessity. A pickup truck catches my eye, as it has an emblem on the hood that eludes most car experts; it is a statue of a gold panner. I ask the old Vietnam vet (and I'm sorry I forgot your name, my friend) inside if I may take a photo of his gold panner and he says, "Sure, sure." We talk a bit, and at this time I notice a large gray chow next to him on the floor. He says his buddy the gray chow is very rare. His name is Keno, and he gets up to sniff my hand with curiosity, perhaps smelling Calvin, my cat. The vet has long gray hair, and the chow has a long gray mane. I think they were meant to be buddies. He says he hopes the VA will help him with a loan he has been awaiting for, for a long time. He wants to maybe buy some land and breed dogs up near Redding. Sometimes he takes people gold panning, he tells me. I tell him I hope God blesses his plans, and we say goodbye. A short while later I see a sign in the fog saying "Trust Jesus." Thank you—I needed that today too.

At an exit with the illustrious name of Road 27 somewhere near Orland, the sun suddenly comes out. Is this one of Hannah's famous "sucker holes?" Indeed, it seems so, as a few miles later the fog is back, although less heavy. The cat-and-mouse game of fog and sun goes on all the way to Red Bluff, then finally the sun wins! Blue skies and sun now, all the way to Redding. In the distance one can see the top portion of Mount Shasta, covered with snow. I think back to the years long ago when my boys and I used to go fishing and camping near here at Whiskeytown Lake. Great hot summers with lots of trout. I check into my motel; it's time for a nap before the evening reception.

Turtle Bay Exploration Park is an amazing place, with a museum, several galleries, botanical gardens, and the Paul Bunyan Forest Camp, an educational program for kids. It sits right next to the Sundial Bridge—Redding's recent cultural claim to fame—an elegant bridge over the Sacramento River that opened in 2004. After checking in briefly at the reception for the gallery opening tonight, I opt to walk across the beautiful bridge, which was designed by world-renowned Spanish architect and engineer Santiago Calatrava. There are a few fishermen standing in the river, up to their waists in water, backlit by the late afternoon sun, casting their fly-fishing lines. A little dog and its human coming across from the other direction walk very apprehensively over the bridge, which is made mostly of glass—perhaps a bit slippery for those little feet. The gleaming white bridge with its steel cables makes a stark contrast to the deep azure blue sky.

It's time for the reception. The show exhibits a variety of art by artists from the Western States and curious visitors (including myself) make the rounds. While discussing a painting with a woman next to me, I find out that she is not only from the area, but from Whiskeytown, the original town that now sits at the bottom of the lake with the same name. It is nice to chat a bit, as I have no friends or family here to share this event with this time. The small buffet outside has garnered an attentive audience and I join them briefly before wandering around in the museum a bit. In one room there is an enormous fish tank from floor to ceiling with fish from the Sacramento River in it, among them salmon and trout. One bright pink fish lazily floats in the upper portion of the tank, the last rays of sun falling through the skylight on top of the tank making the pink even more pink. The rest of the museum has numerous exhibits about the logging and frontier days of the West, as well as a replica of a valley oak in the main room, with roots going down through a glass floor that you can walk on. This is really a well-designed, visually appealing museum.

After saying goodbye to the curator and director, I cross a small wooden bridge—still decorated with Christmas lights—back to the parking lot towards downtown Redding. Tonight is "Art Walk" and I stop at a few buildings to look at some of the work. Dinner beckons at Lumberjack's, a restaurant with a giant lumberjack outside. I opt for a small dinner special, as I imagine the regular portions must be huge judging by the advertisement outside. A still quite-large plate with ribs arrives, and the evening entertainment consists of watching a TV screen on which a chainsaw log-cutting contest can be seen. Imaginative, one must admit—although a nightmare for all trees. Back at the motel, the tail-end portion of the old movie Ghostbusters puts me to sleep.

What a surprise in the morning, the fog has engulfed Redding too. Taking full advantage of the motel's amenities, I go from spa to pool, to spinner bike, to pool, to shower. At the pool I talk with the caretaker about fishing in the area. He tells me he used to catch fish when he went with his grandpa, but when he was alone the fish ignored him. Much in the same vein, I tell him about my son Patrick, who just has to hang a pole in the water for the fish to bite, whereas the trout usually laugh at me—the occasional one I do catch is most likely the one who has been laughing too hard. After leaving the keys to the room at the motel office, I opt to drive to Turtle Bay one more time. As I walk across the Sundial Bridge, fog rises from the river. Dozens of fishermen in boats and in waders have come here in the early morning to catch hungry fish. On the other side of the river is the botanical garden, through part of which I stroll a bit. It must be beautiful come spring. Now, in January, there is almost nothing in bloom. A sign announcing "Rattlesnake habitat, watch your step" encourages a rather quick departure. OK, breakfast time, courtesy of a motel coupon for Lumberjack's, the same destination as last night. It is worth noting that the TV shows women running over rotating logs this time. Equality for all.

OK, Mr. Kotuku, 245 miles to go, and without detours this time. Take me home, please.

Right Side, Left Side
July 2011

Several months ago I discovered Florentine cookies at a Peet's Coffee store, a favorite cookie since my youth in Germany. Mind you, only select Peet's have them, and only on certain days. Detective work and persistence is in order to make the necessary acquisition. The reader may question the word "necessary," but that is his or her privilege. My local Peet's does not carry Florentine cookies and, despite repeated pleas and an e-mail to corporate, results are not forthcoming. Thus it becomes necessary to frequent more than one store. This morning life is good: there are two cookies left and a happy cookie and café latte customer emerges triumphantly from the store.

The last few months there seems to have been a haircut discrepancy whenever I visit the girl who cuts my hair (or what is left of it). Finder's fee is what my dad called it when he went to a barber. In any case, to expand on the mundane, apparently a small section on the back of my head near the middle was apparently not straight, or so I was told. Jeanne, the hair stylist, remarked that perhaps I had cut it unknowingly while shaving. I offered another possibility: perhaps Calvin, my cat, was gnawing at me at night unbeknownst to me. This possibility seemed remote, however. A neighbor suggested that perhaps the mistake was a cover-up when I went to get my hair cut, which resulted in laughing protest on Jeanne's part. So after today's haircut it was proposed that on my next visit we will both look in the second mirror at the back of my head, normally invisible to me, to settle the matter once and for all.

Third stop of the day, a visit to my acupuncture doctor—always a welcome relief for the back. As I was lying on my stomach, probably resembling an overgrown porcupine, I overheard a conversation between a customer and Dr. Ou. The customer apparently wanted some herbs for her dog, and was describing symptoms of great distress on the part of her dog, which had apparently managed to catch a chipmunk and devour said same. I had to restrain myself from laughing. Dr. Ou played along, I'm guessing, as he was mentioning several different herbs.

Heading home, I packed a small bag for the night and said good-bye to Calvin. He was to spend the night alone with my neighbor Bill to feed him while his normal food-supplier was on his way to Santa Cruz to see an anticipated concert.

Middle of July Bay Area drizzle and fog. Where highway 880 turns into 17 in Los Gatos the blue sky wins and sun lavishes the red, pink, and white oleanders that grow on the freeway divider. Such a lovely reminder of summer.

As I climb the hill on 17 towards Santa Cruz, I see a sign for a reptile show on a telephone pole—the location eludes me at the moment. A half a mile later there is another sign for a gun show at the same location. One hopes that both events will occur during different times. A few miles later the Pied Piper exterminator advertises his services in the vicinity of Scott's Valley. Traveling can be so educational.

My radio dial is set to 107 oink 5, or KPIG, as it is known in the area. Blues music floats through the car as a high fog can be seen over the Pacific in the distance. I check into my downtown hotel and unpack. I have a few hours before the concert starts, which

I will put to good use to explore and photograph. Santa Cruz has that summer feel to it. Vacancy signs have the "No" part lit and pastel motels and houses bask in the afternoon warmth. Near the boardwalk I pass a store, contemplating the purchase of a pair of flip-flops. I should have bought some, as my aching feet later argue with me. After an hour or two of walking I return to my hotel and take full advantage of the Jacuzzi. Unfortunately there is no pool. Read the fine print, Mr. Online Customer!

After a 20-minute nap, I head downstairs to retrieve Kotuku, my transportation on this trip. The little Honda CR-V finds a parking place downtown. We are both surprised by the 8 p.m. time on the meter. Greedy little things, one might add. A few blocks away down the Jazz Alley is the Kuumbwa Jazz Center, a lovely small venue with good views of the stage and, as it turns out, good food too. I should have waited and not had those chicken strips. An announcer walks on stage and tells us Airto will be a bit late and that there will be free chips and salsa, a welcome companion to the cider I just ordered.

Airto Moreira and his daughter and son-in-law's band arrives. With his usual sense of humor he says, "We are from Brazil, so we are not late." The show is off to a good start. Airto's daughter explains that she has talked her dad into playing tonight with them. It's a great set mixed with the kids' modern hip-hop music and Airto's masterful percussion. I am grateful I get to see him again, and a mere five feet away. My seat neighbor has come all the way from Monterey not to miss it. After Airto's daughter announces it's his 70th birthday celebration Airto comments, "Seventy is not easy, you know. Every morning I have to make tough decisions. Do I get up on the right side or on the left side of the bed?" The audience is

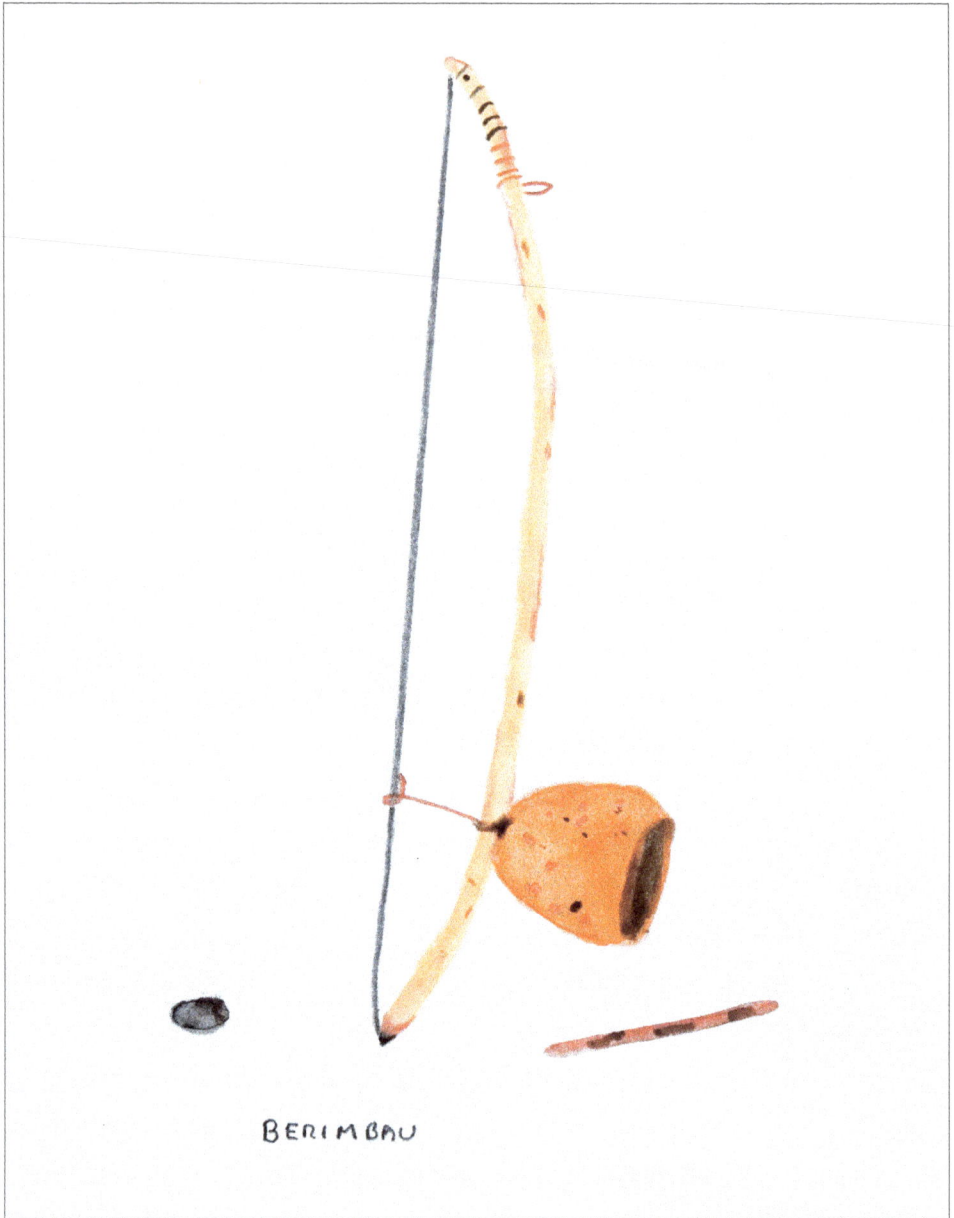

BERIMBAU

very much amused. At intermission my neighbor gets a tambourine autographed and I get to thank Airto for all the years of great music. Since 1974, come to think of it, when I immigrated to California. The second set is just as good, if not better. I always marvel at the variety of percussion instruments he has; this time a squeaking toy frog is among them. After an encore the room slowly empties as people walk happily into the warm summer night.

Fog the next day! Breakfast is not bad: a variety of healthy foods, as well as some waffles. After a waffle and armed with a banana, an apple, a yogurt, and a muffin I make my exit—or should I say escape?

Packed and loaded, Kotuku and I drive through downtown and then park at the pier. It's a quiet walk to the end: fog drifting above, seafood suppliers delivering to restaurants, gulls keeping a watchful eye on things. The sea lions that are normally abundant and noisy under the pier are missing this morning. I see an old VW Vanagon with an Arizona license plate. The plate says "historical" vehicle. That would seem a bit more than debatable. Back in Kotuku we meander along the sea, headed south a bit, to parts of Santa Cruz I have not seen before. The waves today are more than plentiful as hundreds of surfers are either in the ocean already or changing on shore to enter the water. A kid on a skateboard passes me "walking" his dog, a pit bull that seems enthralled by the rapid pace. Santa Cruz turns into Capitola, also a beach town. It sits sort of in a valley and is in full summer mode. Sleepy beachgoers are emerging from their seaside rooms, the gulls are awaiting breakfast, and the waves roll in and out beckoning for surfboards. Lazy summer. Back in Santa Cruz I have some fast-food Chinese, a poor choice, I might add, but no one to blame but yours truly. At a nursery across the street a calandrinia spectabilis and an I-lost-the-tag plant find their way to the trunk to adorn the garden at home. Speed control set for Highway 17 downhill, it's time to go home.

No doubt my extended absence will be duly noted by a certain feline once I return, questioning my whereabouts. As a friend refreshed my memory: Dogs have masters, cats have servants.

Schnukiputzi turns French
September 2011

The big green bag is packed. Included inside is a twenty-pound heavy-duty yellow extension cord that my son Patrick has asked me to bring up to Portland with me. I would love to see the expression on the face of the X-ray machine operator at the airport when he sees the contents of the bag. I think my cat Calvin senses something; he is very affectionate this morning. Sorry, buddy, it's solitary confinement for you for the next ten days. After placing all the indoor plants in the shower and turning it on briefly to soak them (fake rain, they mutter, I'm sure), I shut the valve off. This will be their temporary semi-tropical home. I gather up the rest of my stuff and my neighbor Bill gives me a ride to Oakland Airport.

It's Sunday morning and the terminal is nearly empty as the passengers walk across the tarmac to reach the steps leading up to the front door of a new Bombardier Turbo-Prop airplane. After finding my assigned seat close to the rear of the aircraft I head towards the room of rest, only to discover there is none—at least not here in the rear of the plane. The flight attendant smiles and says it's located in the front, but when we land, the rear door of the plane will also be a second exit, so look on the bright side: easier departure. Maneuvering towards the front I find the only restroom, although it's impossible to stand up in it. I look around for the sink, but there is none! Exiting, I inquire of the second flight attendant about the missing sink. She replies that they build some airplanes this way and that the crew don't like it much either. Strange indeed, to say the least. Perhaps an engineer could better explain what seems to be an unnecessary omission. With surprising acceleration the turbo-prop gains altitude. It is quiet above the clouds too—

PIZZA

unusual for an aircraft of this kind.

It is over 90°F when we land in Portland, a warm welcome indeed after a cold foggy summer in the Bay Area. After retrieving my bag and taking a short ride on a shuttle bus, I make the acquaintance of my rental car, a nondescript white one, with a Florida license plate. That should put me in the tourist category alongside my fellow motorists here in Oregon. One hopes the Oregonian drivers will exhibit patience towards the Floridian the license plate wrongly identifies me to be. My newly acquired GPS directs me towards Patrick's place of employment. The flight came in early, and Patrick calls to tell me to drive slowly so that we can meet there at the same time, as he has not left for work yet. I ask him if he is hungry, and after receiving a yes, which I kind of figured, I manage to coax the location of a Burgerville out of the GPS, which it promptly steers me towards. Two cheeseburgers later, the destination is once again Lucca, the restaurant where Patrick works. On a side street I see a homemade bike with a flat carrying tray built into it between the wheels, kind of a scooter-bike hybrid. An unusual contraption, but what is even more amusing is that the rider is transporting a microwave oven on the platform. One can only wonder.

After a big hug, and then eating the aforementioned cheeseburgers, Patrick introduces me to his coworkers. It seems they have a good crew here. Patrick makes a mushroom pizza with an egg in the middle, which I take with me as a present for Patrick and Sanae, my friends with whom I will be staying. I hope you have an easy shift tonight, my boy. See you tomorrow.

Arriving in Beaverton, at my friends' house, we have a nice chat along with the pizza, which quickly disappears. Their two cats, Mikan and Bella, are nowhere to be seen. It usually takes them quite a bit to acclimate to strangers, although I think they should remember me, considering they slept on my tummy when they were kittens. My friend Patrick suggests going out for dinner. I'm surprised as we just ate, but I think he considers the pizza a snack. We drive to their favorite Chinese place nearby for dinner. Although it's now early evening, the dashboard gauge, trying to justify its existence, brags about a still-high current temperature, which one needs to take with a grain of salt, considering the sun is shining through the window on it. As is so common with Chinese food, several boxes with leftovers leave the restaurant with us. Sanae still wants to buy a few groceries, so we stop at a huge supermarket nearby. Patrick waits in the front, and I forage through the aisles in search of ice cream, and triumphantly return with two flavors of sherbet: raspberry and sauvignon-berry—for consumption over the next few days, in case you are wondering about gluttony. At home, Patrick and I watch a Food Network show on TV about a bunch of food trucks traveling the country vying for prizes—an interesting TV and culinary concept. It's been a long day; good night.

In the morning I find Bella on the balcony, looking at birds. The balcony is a favorite spot of hers, and one she doesn't get to frequent too often. Mikan, meanwhile, is in the kitchen with Patrick, attempting to get "crunchies" for breakfast. Thus we finally meet too, Mr. Orange and White.

My son Patrick calls me and, after grabbing the yellow extension cord, I head over to his and his girlfriend Hannah's apartment, which I have not seen before. Patrick fixes a nice breakfast of leftover potatoes and eggs, along with some good, hot coffee. We then wander down into the basement storage area, where he shows me his work-space and storage unit. He has assembled a table for whale-bone carving, a skill he learned in New Zealand. There is a recently acquired wooden tool chest and bikes racked to the wall up on their front wheels. The smell and lattice-work of the basement reminds me of my uncle's place in Germany from my childhood. The apartment building is quite large with maybe 16 units in it. It is also located conveniently, or perhaps dangerously, close to a Burgerville.

We decide to take a walk around the neighborhood. Patrick and Hannah live in Ladd's Addition, a neighborhood in Portland that is known for its diagonal street pattern. As we exit the apartment building, we spot a cat in the basement window, which runs away from the windowsill it had been sitting on, into the apartment, as I try to approach. Patrick tells me that he and Hannah have a game where they count cats, to see who can get the most. This one, however, is off limits, as it is seen every day. The main street here is beautiful, flanked by huge old trees on both sides as one sees in France, or Alleenstrasse, as we call them in Germany. Bicycles whiz by, as this road is a main thoroughfare for them. It is fun to see the different houses and building styles. Patrick sees a cat: 1:0.

At the corner of the next block we come to, two huge—no, make that gargantuan—speakers with a "free" sign on them, along with a cabinet and an old tape deck, catch Patrick's eye. I should explain that he is known to some as the king of Craig's List regarding freebies, so need I say more? "No, Patrick, no, Patrick, no, Patrick."

"But they are cool, I bet someone's wife made him get rid of them, and we are the lucky finders."

Two older gentlemen walk by, and one of them suggests, "Van Halen would sound pretty good cranked up all the way on those." All right, my boy, put one on my shoulder and you grab the other one. Heavy behemoth is still an understatement for these things. Inside the apartment, Patrick hooks them up, and boy do they work. Mission accomplished. Mr. Van Halen, we are ready for you.

After this unexpected find, and brief setback to our walk, we meander through the neighborhood once again. Sun filters lazily through the tall green canopy covering the entire street. At some of the junctions, rose gardens have been planted. Between the main streets, narrow alleys wind along the backs of the houses.

This is a fun place to explore. Sunflowers turn happily in the sun.

On the other side of the apartment complex is a lot with a big collection of food trucks. Portland seems to be a breeding ground for them. Most of them are closed for Labor Day, so the crêpe truck has a long line in front of it. After ordering and waiting for a while, we are rewarded with a lemon-curd and cheese crêpe, as I recall, and a milkshake and a smoothie to go with it. Thus armed with lunch, we stroll back to the apartment where we listen to the Giants game on the radio, a subscription Patrick has purchased. It's funny to hear Bay Area advertisements up here in Portland in between innings. After the Giants win, Patrick suggests we go for a drive to a park.

We wind up in Cathedral Park in the St. John neighborhood, under a beautiful steel suspension bridge that towers above us. The St. John Bridge has two 400-foot-tall Gothic towers supporting it; it is the tallest bridge in Portland. The elements have given it that copper-green patina. Below it, the Willamette River rambles by. A teenager is fishing on the wooden pier that extends off the park at the embankment. He tells us that he releases the fish after catching them as his girlfriend doesn't like fish. He has caught a small fish that is floating on its side, and he holds it and splashes water on its gills to revive it to start swimming again. I think he is the kindest, most gentle fisherman I have ever met, and a bit unsuited to the sport, I tend to think. As we wander the park, leaving the hopefully recovering fish, we chance upon the head chef from Lucca, Patrick's restaurant. She is enjoying the day in the park with friends and her dogs. Small world. Strolling to the edge of the park, we pass by an industrial area where a huge ship propeller lies on its side. It must be 20–30 feet in diameter. Just massive, even without a ship attached.

ICE CREAM TRUCK - PORTLAND, OREGON

We plan to meet Hannah at the apartment when she comes back from her trip today, but since there is still a bit of time, we stop for a cup of coffee closer to Portland. The skylights inside the café remind Patrick and me of the "dungeon," a warehouse we lived in when he was a kid. I see an old ice cream truck in the parking lot nearby.

The phone rings, and I hear Hannah telling Patrick, "There is something bigger than me inside the apartment." Uh-oh, the speakers have been discovered. By the time we arrive, she has listened to some music she likes through them; the initial shock seems to have been overcome. Will they stay on as permanent residents? Time will tell. It is so nice to see Hannah-girl, as I call her. She has just returned from a camping trip in eastern Oregon.

Washing up a bit, we leave the apartment, and Patrick starts the cat game again by seeing one. I had forgotten about it. Hannah's eyes scan the neighborhood in search of more. We walk through Ladd's Addition and then a bit further to our dinner destination, St. Jack, a new country-style French restaurant in Portland, where we meet Patrick and Sanae. I think there may have been one or two more cats along the way, but my memory is vague. Dusk approaches, and candles light the warm wooden tables inside the restaurant. The food, which comes little by little during our conversation after we order, ranges from *gratin d'escargots*, to roasted bone marrow, to frog legs (which I did not ask to sample out of respect for Hannah's frog, Scuppers), to mussels, to roasted trout, and steak frites, and is just superb. The crowning touch is a bowl of warm, freshly baked small madeleines. A wonderful evening. Patrick and Sanae head home, and I walk with Patrick and Hannah to their apartment before driving back to Beaverton. As I recall, the cat score may have been tied, or it may have been in Hannah's favor at this point. I do recall seeing one cat dash across an alley under the glow of a streetlight and before I could even think about cats, the word "cat" was yelled at least once, probably twice. Bedtime: speaking of, a comment I heard that made me chuckle, was Hannah's description of Patrick lying down in bed: a starfish taking over.

The next morning, Bella is sitting on the deck again in the morning sunshine, looking on as a blue jay pierces the air making its presence

STAR FISH

known, as they do so well. The plan is to explore a bit of downtown Portland today, but before that, the GPS finds the local AAA office in Beaverton for me. It is probably a bit insulted, as I plan to get some maps that fold out, to get a better overview. As I collect my maps, one of which encompasses the Columbia River region, the lady behind the counter remarks, "The Columbia River was carved out by giant icebergs. A famous professor at the University has proven that—he is an expert." Not that I had solicited this information. It always amuses me how people matter-of-fact believe this stuff. Considering our limited written history as mankind, some nonetheless believe they are experts regarding what they think happened millions of years ago. God must be chuckling.

Parking downtown on SW Park Avenue, another wonderful tree-lined street, I walk by the Portland Art Museum and notice they have a special exhibit of classic cars. I make a mental note of it, as my friend Patrick loves cars. At the Visitor Information Center in Pioneer Courthouse Square, a gentleman with a heavy Irish accent gives me an assortment of brochures and tells me not to miss visiting the courthouse across the street. I have to pass through a metal detector, which is staffed by two rather corpulent men assuring safety of the building. One of them is a U.S. marshall I believe. He asks for my identification, studies my driver's license, and then benevolently tells me this is the oldest courthouse west of the Mississippi, commissioned by Abraham Lincoln. It is also on the National Register of Historic Places. He also tells me most of the rooms are accessible, but not to disturb anyone should they be working. Lastly I am advised about the glass cupola at the top of the building, which I am told has a stupendous view. The halls are paneled with wood from floor to ceiling, and the hallways are very quiet, the carpets soaking up what little sound may penetrate this well constructed building. It has a historic feel to it: elegant, formal, from a different era. An old metal elevator takes me upstairs, and after a last flight of stairs, I come to the cupola. It is as hot as a greenhouse on this summer day; huge glass windows on all sides make the eyes squint from the bright light engulfing the room. The view is indeed panoramic, although buildings crop up on all sides, partially obscuring it. I was also told that there was, at one point, a clear view of the Willamette River from here, in order to observe and tax shipping traffic. On the bottom floor again, the temperature is at least 20–30 degrees cooler. I admire a few more rooms, and then make my way to the exit.

After lunch, I explore the edges of the Pearl District near the river.

One part is especially worth seeing: Tanner Park, about a square block, where wetland habitat has been restored, surrounded by modern-day architecture. A bit tired, I rest on a bench in the park, and sit very still as several sparrows come to a small trickle of a stream flowing over some rocks and, gradually tiptoeing closer, proceed to take a bath, ruffling their feathers and shaking off the water drops with delight and abandon. Such graceful little birds. I have to think of the hymn of God telling his children not to worry about what to eat, since he feeds the sparrows too. I stay for a long time to watch the little sparrows; it is so peaceful.

My last stop is the Salmon Street Springs, where the summer fountains bubble with abandon. The sun creates a rainbow on the fountain spray, and kids shriek in delight as they race in and out of the splashing water. I too step into the fountain a little bit, protecting my camera under my arm as I do. I too can't resist the water. A creamsicle at a bike rental booth nearby completes the summer afternoon.

Arriving in Beaverton, I tell Patrick about the auto show, but much to my surprise he has already seen it. Sanae comes home, and we have a mildly seasoned pork tenderloin curry stew that Patrick has cooked up. Delicious.

I meet my son Patrick at his apartment the next morning, and we stroll to the bakery at St. Jack. The croissants and café au lait are excellent. Ah, just like France. *C'est bon*. A few motorcycles are parked in front of the bakery, and our conversation turns to motorcycle and then bicycle talk. Thus inspired we head back to the apartment to watch an episode of Top Gear, the British version, where the three commentators embark on a trip through the desert in Africa. It is very amusing what they go through with their three junk cars to overcome various setbacks and obstacles. Afterwards I suggest to Patrick that we go see the classic car exhibit at the Portland Art Museum.

At the museum, I am able to purchase a senior ticket for myself, amused that I am considered to be one at the mere age of 55, but hey, I'll take the discount. They have some incredible cars inside. Our favorite is a jet-black and canary yellow Bugatti with a tan ostrich leather interior. This isn't just a car; it is a work of art. A deep blue teardrop-shaped Talbot is also magnificent. Well, to be honest, they were all pretty fine specimens, from the James Bond car to the Pan-America Porsche. Boys will be boys.

Lunch is in a small hole-in-the-wall downtown where, besides soup and grilled cheese, I have a milkshake, with one of the ingredients being purple haze syrup. Hmmm, I wonder what kind of music the owner likes?

This is definitely a car day. On the way back, we drive past a neighborhood that has not one but two old Citroëns parked behind each other. One is a rusted-out immovable bucket of bolts, but the DS 21, that classic automobile with the first rear-wheel hydraulic lift, could be restored with much love and patience. Patrick also sees an International pickup truck with a crane in the back, for sale, something I have hopefully talked the King of Craig's list out of purchasing. Pay back your loans first, my son. After using Patrick's laptop to book a hotel for the next few nights, we say goodbye for the day, as Patrick has to work, and I head for a nap in Beaverton. Equal distribution of labor? I guess I still sleep a lot, since my back surgery last year. Wait a minute, I should expand on the hotel: Patrick had mentioned there was a motel he had seen in his neighborhood that he thought was probably reasonably priced. They wanted around $70 a night, we found out after he called them. Well, after our trip to the museum, we drove by there to take a look, and I must say a Roach Motel seemed more appealing to me than this sad excuse for lodgings, which will remain nameless. I then searched a website that specializes in discount rates and found a three-star hotel near the Convention Center for less than the motel we saw. A very easy decision.

After my nap, I discuss the cars we saw with my old friend Patrick, and suggest we go back to St. Jack for dinner again tonight, but he has something else in mind. I'm stubborn that way; if I really like a place I will go back again and again. Sanae comes home from work, and we drive downtown. I forget the name of the place, but it was a French restaurant too. The one interesting thing Patrick pointed out was that at the back wall of the restaurant robbers had attempted to break into the jewelry store next door, through heavy brick walls, but failed in their attempt. The broken brick segments, and their folly, was still on view for the dining audience to enjoy. The hostess sits us in a booth. Unfortunately, sitting directly behind me is an imbecile who not only is working on her laptop, but also shooting off her mouth nonstop. Annoying, to say the least. It's beyond me how you can bring a laptop to a nice restaurant. Savage. Thank God two guitarists appear from their break and proceed to play some beautiful classical music, silencing the noise behind us. There is a blackboard next to me with today's specials, and Patrick wonders what I am doing as I glance towards the hostess, waiting for her to turn her head, and then turning my head to look at the specials board. I have to do this several times, until the hostess finally turns her head. My intention is to turn "Tillamook Cheese" into "Tillamoo Cheese" by erasing the last letter, but my attempt is foiled by the heavy-duty chalk. At least I tried. The food is good, but not great like at St. Jack. Patrick is ticked off, because the half chicken he ordered is more of a pigeon in size. I have the trout, and ask our waitress to pack the fish remains for me, and the head for the cats at home. It's a nice warm evening for a stroll, but Patrick seems a bit tired and we decide to go home. In Beaverton again, Mikan and Bella don't even give the fish head a second look when it is unwrapped and presented. Call yourselves cats, will you? After some blackberry Sauvignon sherbet we say good night again.

I had bought a few Kaiser rolls the day before in the Pearl District— I wonder where they get that name from? To me they are simply poppy-seed rolls. One of them makes my acquaintance this morning, along with his friends cream cheese and butter. That reminds me of the time when my sons used to question me incredulously, "You put butter under brie on your bread?" Yup. I think that was during the cholesterol hype time period. Then it's time to pack. I'm leaving for a few days, to give my friends a little space. As I walk past the kitchen, the fish-head is still staring at me from the bowl, untouched. A sad sight indeed.

The destination today is Mount St. Helens, the site of the infamous volcanic eruption in 1980. After leaving Beaverton and crossing over the Willamette River, I-5 takes me north over the Columbia River into Washington State. Here I see two hulking logging trucks simultaneously: one is carrying huge raw logs and barreling along the freeway; the other one is carrying the finished product in square form at a bit slower pace. Nice to have a visual comparison. Mr. GPS advises me to continue on I-5 north into Washington State and then

SMOKED TROUT

remains quiet until we get to Castle Rock, where we turn right, and the drive begins to turn scenic. There has been a fire near Mt. Hood in Oregon for the past week, and smoke is still drifting north. At the moment it is not bad here; blue sky is to be seen. I drive past a blue lake, then marshlands and wetlands, as trees begin to populate both sides of the road. Signs tell the passer-by what year the trees were planted. Green dots on the map don't lie about scenery.

Mr. GPS, however, remains ignorant of the dots. I stop at almost every lookout point to gaze into the valley below. It is now getting hazy, and some of the moon-like barren landscape can be seen in the distance. At one point, a sign advertises elk viewing below. I park and walk around for a bit. Insects that kind of look like jumping crickets catch my attention. When they land, however, they spread out butterfly-like wings.

Returning to the car, a fellow traveler grins at me and asks "Seen any elk?"

"Nope." I grin back.

The end of the road is at the Johnston Ridge Observatory. As I exit the car, I am surrounded by bugs, bugs, and more bugs. Small, and they don't really bite, I think, but annoying nonetheless, like meter-maids. The walk to the Visitor Center is uphill. I check in with my National Park pass and head back out to look around. The skies are now gray and ashy. A hazy, partially snow-capped Mt. St. Helens can be seen in the distance. Bizarre looking trees, remnants from the great eruption, are visible everywhere here, at over 4,000 feet of elevation. After a climb around the top of the Visitor Center area, I make my way back indoors, tired of the bugs. Inside is a large scale model of the mountain and lakes surrounding it, with LEDs lighting up and explaining the circumstances of the eruption. Fun to look at, and play with. In another section, there is a spot you can stand to experience a simulated earthquake. An old hat for a Californian, but I enjoy watching the other tourists having a good time with it. After a short wait, the movie theater opens up, and we take our places. After it gets dark, the drama unfolds. Live footage on a panoramic screen shows the awesome power of the 1980 eruption, narrated perhaps a bit over-dramatically. To see massive trees broken like matchsticks and the lava and ash cascading down the mountain is overwhelming. At the end of the show, the curtain rises and Mt. St. Helens can be seen through glass windows that reach from floor to ceiling. This is a well-conceived building and exhibit.

Exiting the theater, I find the car in the lot and have some leftover trout from the night before for lunch. Yum. No—not the refused uneaten head and bones! Traveling back on the same highway I make a stop at Hoffstadt Bluffs Visitor Center. In front of the building is a semi-demolished news vehicle from 1980. The inside of the Visitor Center is very interesting. A collection of old newspapers hangs in a hallway, a bit yellowed with age, of course. On one of the front pages President Jimmy Carter can be seen touring the damage and promising government relief. Inside the gift shop, I purchase a beautiful colored glass ball, one of many hanging near the window so the light can shine through them. The tag says the glass ball is made by local artists in Seattle, including the use of some of the authentic 1980 ashes. I guess for some this is a selling point, but to me only the color of the glass is important.

The next stop many miles down the road is a small restaurant where I have Patty's homemade strawberry-rhubarb cobbler, with vanilla ice cream, after a suggestion by the waitress that you just can't separate the two. The deck of the restaurant is probably at least 100 feet above the river, which rushes below. Good pit stop. Before reaching I-5 again I drive by a "Starducks" coffee shop sporting a duck logo and advertising espresso. I hope the corporate lawyers of a similar sounding franchise leave them alone.

As Mr. GPS now directs me back to Oregon (not much of a challenge on a long straight road for him, come to think), commuter traffic is congested heading back up into Washington. Mr. GPS finds my hotel, and I check in at the front desk before parking the car. Not only am I given a welcome cookie by the friendly receptionist, but she also gives me a beautiful upgrade on the 12th floor when I ask if she might have something with a view of downtown Portland, as I am a photographer. Thank you. After parking, it's off to the pool for a swim and to stretch after the long day. In the lobby there is a large pitcher of cucumber water, which is thoughtful, and very refreshing.

After resting for a bit, I head to Patrick's restaurant for dinner. The hostess seats me at the counter right where Patrick is preparing pizzas for baking in the wood-fired oven. The chef has come up with a special drink for the night that includes sherbet, which I have one too many of, in addition to the large plate of antipasti, and a pizza, of course. The death blow is a bowl of chocolate dessert. I should know better by now, not to stuff myself, but no. At this point I need to mention that chocolate is my best friend (besides ice cream, of course) and although I am always willing to try something new, the way this was served was revolting. Not only was the chocolate sprinkled with sea salt but olive oil as well. Bread, yes. Steaks, yes. Fish, yes. Chocolate, an emphatic no. The rest of the food was delicious. Lumbering to my hotel, I have a pretty sleepless night, with many TUMS in between trips to the restroom. Stupid, greedy me.

In the morning after a brief swim, I once again head over to Patrick and Hannah's apartment. I have found out how to make my GPS talk in German; rather interesting what these things are capable of these days. Hannah is at work already, and I meet Patrick at the door. I suggest St. Jack for breakfast again, but he wants to go to a place in the neighborhood. After a, to me, much too long walk, and still suffering from sleep deprivation, we arrive. I'm in a grouchy mood, and Patrick tells me, "I don't believe you just said that this restaurant smells within ear shot of the waiter." It turns out the smell is green coffee being roasted. We order a mostly organic corned beef and hash, and a stack of bacon something sandwich.

The coffee is pretty good. The breakfast portions are large and we can't finish and take the leftovers with us. We pass a Monet-like garden in front of a hardware store with an abundance of flowers. It's a summer field of delight. Patrick tells me he much prefers this type of garden rather than the water-guzzling lawns that are so prevalent, and an absurd waste of water in desert regions such as southern California. I am still rather groggy and probably—no, definitely—need a nap, so I drive back to the hotel while Patrick goes to work.

Naps work wonders and, refreshed, I take another swim in the pool and then read the Oregonian, Portland's local paper, in my room. Dinner is at Lucca again. This time Patrick gives me just a plate of antipasti, which he thoughtfully prepares to be non-acidic. The big doofus (me) is learning to eat in moderation. Patrick seems busy tonight, so I say goodbye until tomorrow. I had wanted to invite Hannah for dinner tonight, but she is working.

Departing, I head for—you guessed it—St. Jack. I order an Amaretto and the wonderful small madeleines. A very sweet girl with a warm smile comes to my table, bringing water, and says, "I'm so sorry you don't have a lit candle at your table," and brings me one. A sudden gust of wind had extinguished my candle. The evening is warm and pleasant. It feels like summer in France. A few people have settled in the outside chairs at the tables on the sidewalk. The wind rustles through the leaves of the large trees again. There is a small dog at one of the tables next to me where a couple is sitting. The dog has its head on the ground and seems content. A man approaches the tables. He has a small bulldog on a leash, which he ties to a chair, before going inside to the bar. The other dog's interest is briefly piqued, but he settles back down. As the waiter brings the couple's food, the first dog stands up to beg but is reprimanded, and lies down again reluctantly but obediently. In the meantime, the bulldog has dragged the chair a bit, trying to locate its owner, and has turned the leash into a quasi-jump rope. I admire the other waitress who comes out, carrying more plates, as she elegantly sidesteps the dog and leash in stride without losing a step. The full moon is out now and silver light filters over the tables as the candles flicker and burn lower.

Not enough time for a swim this morning; it's time to pack. I go to the lobby first, to try to find some coffee before checking out. At a counter, there is indeed some to be found. A young boy of about nine or ten tells the girl at the counter that his dad has sent him to the lobby to try to find free coffee. The girl is amused, but tells him the coffee is not free. The boy pulls out a five-dollar bill from his pocket and hands it to her. I look at him and ask if he likes cookies. What a dumb question, of course. I tell him to go to the receptionist and to ask for a goodbye cookie. Since they have hello cookies they surely must have the latter. He is too bashful, however. Too bad. I take the elevator back upstairs and get my stuff and take it to the car. Then I check out and sheepishly ask the receptionist for a goodbye cookie. She gives me a "aren't you a bit too old for this" look but hands over the cookie. Ask and you shall receive.

After buying a three-pack of T-shirts (two of which are black, which I didn't know, as the top one was gray, but they become restaurant uniform T-shirts for Patrick later, so all is well), I drive to the apartment. Hannah's plan for today is a Farmer's Market, but she has changed her mind and wants to go to the beach. I think the frog kite I gave her and the warm weather are the deciding factors. I have some of the leftover hash from yesterday and Hannah makes a delicious berry yogurt drink

After packing we head towards I-5, or should I say Ms. GPS tells us to. Indeed, the GPS has switched gender. I have decided to name the now German female voice of the GPS Schnukiputzi (pronounced Schnookeypootzi), a female term of endearment, which Hannah repeats and pronounces quite well. I must inform both her and Patrick of Schnukiputzi's shortcomings, however, as she refers to I-5 as Eins minus 5 (1 minus 5). Perhaps she is a recent immigrant, not quite adept at translation yet. After about an hour of driving, I have to call her navigation skills into question again. She is proposing to cross back over the Columbia River into Oregon. That seems like backtracking to me. Patrick and Hannah take her side however, and I am outvoted. Sure enough, after crossing the river, we come to a beautiful Oregon highway that parallels the river. I had only gone along the Washington side many, many years ago, and presumed that to be the best route. Schnukiputzi, however, is going for speed not scenery, although this stretch of highway is beautiful too. Our destination is Astoria at the mouth of the river. On the side of the road I see a sign that just cracks me up: "Seoul Food," an imaginative and pun-oriented Korean owner it seems. Meanwhile Hannah is playing a game called "Angry Birds" on her phone in the back seat. She seems to be having a lot of fun, despite occasional mishaps that are vocalized.

As we near Astoria, we encounter a traffic jam that seems to stretch for miles. Hannah is playing with the GPS and suddenly Schnukiputzi turns French, a very different voice than her German counterpart. Of course this all matters very little as we are practically standing still. Three motorcycles in front of us are also part of the stop-and-go. I'm surprised they don't go around on one of the sides available—after all, that is their advantage over cars. Tweedle-dee-tweedle-dum. Progress little by little, from a snail's perspective. On the right side of the road, I see a junky old barn with all kinds of stuff in and around it. The owner has displayed the following sign: "Keep out Theevin son of biches." Add bad grammar to limited vulgar vocabulary and thus is the result—most likely a deterrent, however. The traffic starts up again slowly and we see a tow truck and a damaged vehicle on the side, which has caused the backup.

We are hungry and stop at the Fort George Brewing Company in Astoria and sit down outside, first in the sun, then in the shade. It's still a beautiful warm sunny day, even though not quite as warm as Portland. Patrick orders a spicy burrito (the hot sauce bottle depicts a person with a flame coming out of his mouth—I would not in my wildest dreams even attempt to sample that one), and Hannah and I have the fish and chips, which are made from yellow-fin tuna. Patrick also orders the beer sampler, which is about seven or eight shot glasses of beer, a sensible decision so as not to drink large glasses of each, which would most certainly eliminate him as a driver on the way back. The wooden plate the glasses come on reminds us of a great place near my parents' house where we used to eat "Strammer Max" (a ham and egg sandwich, to keep the translation simple) along with a glass of Schnapps. It was a favorite place for us to go after hot summer garden and farm work in Germany. I order a "Dakota Fanning," a mixture of soda and cranberry juice named after some movie star, I'm told. Not bad, and refreshing. The fish and chips is so-so though, in my opinion. For dessert we walk a few blocks to the Custard King, which is available for sale for a mere $189,000, or as the flyer advertises, "Own a piece of American history." We walk away with a milkshake and a sundae. All is well.

After inquiring directions in a museum, Hannah emerges and we head towards a battery located a bit south on the coast, which she has visited before in the springtime. We park and explore it for a bit, and then head for the beach to fly kites. Once we climb over the dunes a strong wind greets us; the wonderful smell of the sea is in the air. I found a frog kite earlier this year that I saved, which I gave to Hannah, and she puts it together, battling the wind. Patrick is assembling another kite that is bigger; the string stretches out probably twice as far as the frog kite I would guess. In no time the kites ascend into the sky. Patrick is teasing Hannah by trying to push down the frog kite with his bigger kite. They are fun to watch tussling about; it makes my heart glad to see them so happy. This beach is also the site of an old shipwreck, whose partial iron skeletal remains protrude from the sand into the sky. The wreckage must be a good 15 feet tall. The sand beneath my feet feels so good—there is no better feeling than walking on a beach barefoot. I photograph the old shipwreck and stroll along the beach looking at the kites and some kite surfers who are enjoying the day. Glancing back, I see Patrick and Hannah still having fun with their kites.

It's time to head back. We pass a house that has hundreds of floats and buoys hanging on it, a spectacular colorful sight. Coming back into Astoria we see the outline of the massive bridge that spans the Columbia River. On the left side I see an old bicultural VW Bus that has been restored and painted with the stars and stripes of the American flag. Incredible restoration job—someone put a lot of effort into this. We decide to drive across the Astoria Bridge. The main span rises about 200 feet above the river, and was built to withstand 150 mph winds. As we reach the top of the bridge, we can see the lower part of it below, unfolding like a roller coaster. I step on the gas as we descend. Wheeeeeeeeeeeeeeeee! This bridge is awesome. On the other side, we park to take in the view of the Columbia River and the bridge. It's simply breathtaking, the width of the river and the engineering feat to build a bridge to span it. Patrick resorts to his favorite pastime, taking found rocks and balancing them on other rocks. He balances three rocks as if it were nothing. I don't think I could manage a single one. He has the touch. He grins broadly as he and Hannah pose in front of the rocks.

Although no roller coaster this time, it's just as much fun to cross the bridge again. Hannah sees a cat in Astoria. 1:0. Several miles outside of town we make a final pit stop, and Patrick gets some coffee and I buy a pack of Pepperidge Farm goldfish, the original flavor. Hannah didn't know the original flavor existed; it is new to her. The fish start to disappear as Patrick has taken over the driving, and I feed him and Hannah. A CD of the Doobie Brothers music plays for the second time today. Patrick has become a really good driver—courteous, smooth, and easy-going. It's a peaceful night-time ride back to Portland. Just before we reach their apartment, I see a large neon sign at a bar nearby that says "olly odger." These pirates are short a few letters—too much rum, perhaps? Good night, you two

Today is the solemn anniversary of 9-11. I had wanted to attend a service this morning in a nearby church, but I was overtired from the trip yesterday, and didn't wake up until almost noon. Fetching some coffee from the kitchen, I meander to the back porch. Bella has managed to follow me, cautiously, and is walking along the top of the railing headed toward a plant. She spies a spider web with the spider right in the middle of its woven realm. The spider makes a hasty retreat into the flowerpot as the cat nose approaches.

A wise decision on its part. Bella is plainly disappointed. It's supposed to get to 94°F today, one of the warmest days of the year, and it is hot already—wonderful. Patrick and Hannah are coming over today to watch the 49er–Seahawks game on TV with us. I ask Big Patrick about getting some stuff for the BBQ later, but he tells me it's covered. After a 49er win, with one lone Seahawks fan being a good sport, my friend Patrick proceeds to BBQ. Sanae makes a really good salad. A very filling and delicious dinner. Hannah and Patrick leave for home and I go to sleep early again.

Today is "dough-day" at Lucca. The chef has invited me to attend, and I bring my camera to document the day, and to reciprocate later with photos. Patrick is already there when I arrive. The visitors are two people from Italy: a representative from a flour company and a professional pizza maker. There are several people from restaurants and suppliers in attendance, as well as the staff of Lucca, of course. To describe the intricate and precise process of dough making and storage is a bit beyond my capabilities, but a few memories that stick out: the pizza chef demonstrating the dough by pulling it out so thin that it looks like a translucent spider web with the dough still not breaking, and one of the attendees remarking, "This isn't surgery, folks," when he sees the intense look of concentration on the faces of some of the people attending the demonstration. What is also quite interesting is the fact that the use of a wood-fired oven turns out to be just aesthetics; the flour company representative explains that the smoke actually spirals up, and never touches the pizza. At the end of the demonstration that includes many finished edible delights, the chef brings out a bottle of rosé to toast the day.

Patrick cleans up, and we leave to meet for Happy Hour at—where

KOI

else?—St. Jack. Patrick orders a drink made with Ricard, that wonderful summer drink from Marseille. I settle for ice water, and we have some fresh-baked bread with pork rillettes and a bowl of olives. I order a bowl of the small madeleines and we each have just a few, as I intend them to be for Hannah. We return to Patrick's apartment where I see some dahlias in a vase, and I find out that today is their two-year anniversary since they met. I'm glad I brought the madeleines. Hannah gives Patrick a pair of flip-flops—one for each year—adorable. Hannah then shows me video footage on her laptop of her as a kid, maybe when she was four or five years old. It is hilarious—she is brushing her teeth and doing a good job, and then is told it's time for bed and goes into a hysterical, probably five-minute-long, temper tantrum at the prospect of retiring. What a kid, and what endurance! OK, time to leave, and let them enjoy their time together. I should be going anyway too, as I have invited Patrick and Sanae for dinner to thank them for their hospitality.

We have been here before, a few years back, at the Culinary Academy of Portland. They have a fixed price four-course dinner and lunch menu as part of the school in their dining room. Not only are they super reasonable, but the food is superb. Two items that stand out this evening are the cauliflower puree and crème brûlée, both exquisite. We return to our cars and drive home. As I make a turn and proceed down a tree-lined street, I have to brake as a squirrel runs across the street and sits down smack in the middle of the road directly in front of my car. I have to honk at it twice before it moves. What audacity! He must think he is Supersquirrel. Where is the cape, dude?

Departure day and the weather is cool and overcast today, perhaps to acclimate me for the Bay Area again. I pack and say goodbye to Patrick, having said goodbye to Sanae the night before, as she went to work this morning already. I gas up in Beaverton, enjoying the full-service and windshield cleaning, and Mr. GPS, back to his original factory voice, steers me to a Portland must for me, the Portland Japanese Garden, but not before we stop for an avocado bacon cheese sandwich and coffee—sorry Mr. GPS, nothing for you.

The driver of the cart that takes people up to the garden advises us to please turn off our cell phones so that others may experience the quietness and peace of the garden. Nicely done, although that should probably be common sense. After passing the entrance I stop at the main building where I pause to look over the scorched dried islands in the middle of the sea, or what the raked gravel and the dried grass patches in between it are supposed to represent. Maple trees in the distance frame the sea. The shutters and walls of the main building exude an aromatic wood smell. I sit and let it soak in with all my senses. In a lower portion of the garden, the trickling streams meander over the rocks, past azaleas, in a damp richness of soil. Near the Zen rock garden, which several employees of the garden are cleaning, a couple of small kids rambunctiously roam about, being kids, of course, and receiving occasional reprimands from their parents. In the lower portion of the garden, where the large pond and iris are, several koi glide effortlessly through the water, flashing orange and red, which looks especially beautiful in the shadow portions, near the embankment. As always, I can watch these fish forever. The small shop near the gate has a large metal bell hanging from its entrance, deep red in color. I ring it and a long deep sound drifts through the garden. I am reminded of the countryside church bells that ring on Sunday mornings in Germany. I love this place. Forsaking the cart that brought us up, I make my way down the path among the maple trees that are still green, before they change to their bright clothes for the fall.

The rose gardens at the bottom of the hill are my next destination. A myriad of colors, the roses beckon me to smell, touch, and enjoy their beauty before they fade with autumn. Sometimes just a few petals on the ground can delight the eye. A few insects are still busy going about their work in some of them. From bright fireworks colors to the subtle watercolor palette, this garden is the pride of the "City of Roses." I purchase something I have never seen before: rose tea.

It's getting toward lunch, and then rental-car drop-off time. Mr. GPS tells me to go over a bridge, unaware of the fact that there is a long backup on it, which I can see from below. Ignoring his suggestion I drive on. Re-calculating, he tells me, and I ignore him again at the next bridge, which is closed for temporary repairs. Bridge number three seems to satisfy both of us, and we cross the Willamette River.

Now for a final stop at St. Jack. Those pork rillettes were so good they beckon for seconds, and the fresh fig jam with baguettes looks good too, complemented by a glass of French Grenache wine. Looking through a half-full glass, I notice the intersection here seems to be a freeway for bicycles. Some riders casually turn the corner; others lean at severe angles, taking the corner with breakneck speed. Some stop at the stop sign when going straight; others do not. I don't think I have ever seen this many bicycles outside of Europe. It's non-stop it seems, pun intended. My glass is close to empty now, as the wind whistles through the leaves telling me it's time to go.

Once more driving through the canopy of trees of Ladd's Addition, the airport edges ever closer. Mr. GPS can't find the street I tell him to find, and we are lost. Driving by instinct and saying a short prayer, I find the vicinity of the airport and then the road to the terminal. From there I follow the route from memory (luckily it works this time) that the shuttle bus that dropped me off took when I arrived. A bit late, but still on time for the flight, I get to the gate, having checked a much lighter bag. I get a surprised look from a passer-by who hears my backpack talking. I have stuffed Mr. GPS in it, who apparently is quite lost and perturbed by this fact, and makes this known in no uncertain terms. Since his keyboard is also faulty, as I have discovered, he will be exchanged upon my return.

For his replacement I hope to find one with a more pleasant voice who can keep the re-calculating stuff to him/her-self. Entry is at the rear of the aircraft, and a trip up to the washroom reveals another sink-less cubby-hole. Time to go home, to release the four-footed prisoner.

Cat Carriers
Christmas 2011

Calvin slept next to my pillow last night. I guess he sensed that something was up when I brought the large green travel bag downstairs. Don't worry, my friend, you will be fed while I'm gone.

I love short flights like this one to Portland. Exiting the terminal, the temperature feels about 10–15 degrees cooler than when I left the Bay Area. Hello there! Wake up! As I wait for Patrick to pick me up, a traffic cop is encouraging cars waiting at the curb to depart the terminal unless they are loading passengers. He is very nice about it, and I'm more than surprised by this, being used to hearing harsh barking and shrill whistles at the Bay Area airports for the same minor infraction. While I am waiting, we chat together about a small Fiat that has just pulled away, having been asked (nicely) to circle once more. Surprisingly, Fiats are being sold in the U.S. once again. I inform him that the acronym *Fehler in allen Teilen* in German stands for "failure in all parts," a term I learned recently from a customer. The traffic director is amused.

The black Subie pulls up. Hey, my boy, so good to see you. I'm so happy to be able to come up for Christmas. We reach Patrick and Hannah's apartment, where Patrick shows me the used Toyota T100 pickup that is parked outside, which he and Hannah have just bought together. A practical investment in a multi-use vehicle for someone good with his hands and tools. The wheels and tires are huge; the truck sits up high, even taller than my 23-year-old Chevrolet of distinction.

I remember the cat counting game that Patrick and Hannah played in the fall when I visited them, and I see the same orange four-footed basement apartment–window dweller I saw back in September. As I approach the window, he runs off by jumping inside onto the floor of the apartment. Scaredy-cat. But of course he doesn't count for the game anyway, as he is an inside cat and seen every day.

We have lunch at the Burgerville right across the street from the apartment, which is decorated very festively for Christmas with a multitude of red and green balloons. Inside the apartment, the Christmas tree that I'd seen in a picture is missing. I'm told it has been transported to the vegetable farm that Patrick is house-sitting for a week.

Patrick has a surprise for me. He has discovered a German culinary specialty store nearby; walking inside it indeed feels like a store back home. They have everything from toothpaste to chocolate to beer. We pick up some Graubrot, Schinken and Teewurst (bread, ham, and a type of sausage), as well as a few other items for consumption over the next few days. A sardine would feel very comfortable inside the store, as it is jam-packed in every aisle, corner, and doorway with last-minute before-Christmas shoppers. The cashiers look overwhelmed.

Patrick heads to work at his restaurant job, and I am given a list of additional grocery items to purchase. It's a grim sight in the Fred Meyer parking lot. Battles and fights for scarce parking spaces, even on the upper level—all in the spirit of Christmas, of course. A car in front of me backs out, and I wait to enter as another car in front of me tries to back up to steal the spot. I learned this lesson the hard way in San Francisco, so that won't fly, my friend. Nonetheless, I wish you good spot hunting. Inside the store, I find a very nice bottle of New Zealand white wine, which I intend to surprise Patrick with, as he has traveled to New Zealand. Also in the cart are four huge boxes of kosher salt—but more on that later. Exiting the parking lot mayhem, where extra security guards are on duty now to deal with the unruly masses, the groceries are brought back safely to the apartment.

Hannah calls and tells me she and her mom, Joan, will be at the apartment in about half an hour. It has gotten dark outside as we load up the rest of the stuff we need to bring, and then we proceed to caravan to the farm. The commuter traffic around Portland seems to have gotten quite a bit worse. I'm the last car of the caravan (Patrick's Subie) I am later told that I was easily recognizable in the rear-view mirror(s) as one of the headlights on the Subie points skyward. As we arrive in the dark, we are greeted by two big friendly barking dogs (retrievers, I think). Inside the house, we sample some apple cider with berries, which Joan has brought with her. It is exquisite. Hannah roasts a chicken for dinner, to which I contribute a sauce I learned in a cooking class at the Alliance Française in San Francisco. Properly nourished, we play a game at the table called Scattergories. It's really quite simple to play: you pick a category, write down the letters A-Z on a sheet of paper, and then you try to make a word with each letter. Our category for tonight happens to be candy. Needless to say, different generations have different knowledge, and the results are interesting and amusing. I dispute various forms of chocolate falling into the candy category, although Joan seems very amused by her attempts to fill in the blanks in this manner. Patrick finally comes home from work and has some chicken too. The cider is reheated. We then find our sleeping accommodations in the house. There is a very interesting room upstairs; it is empty except for piles of onions drying on the floor. It smells very onion soupy. I have heard of church onion towers but this is ridiculous. Unfortunately, the dogs outside believe there is something to bark about, so sleep comes a bit late.

A blood-red sky briefly wakes me in the early morning, but I turn over and go back to sleep, which elicits the comment "call yourself a photographer" from Patrick later on. Stumbling downstairs I meet Joan, who is drinking tea. I can't find the coffee despite a thorough search. There is an old-fashioned coffee grinder attached to the edge of the dining room table, so it has to be here somewhere. The mystery is cleared as Patrick comes downstairs and tells us the people who live here keep their coffee in the freezer. That's the last place I would look for it. Hannah makes some delicious scrambled eggs for breakfast, and Patrick makes coffee—freshly ground, of course. The aroma of coffee beans fills the dining room air and floats into the kitchen. I meet one of the four animal residents of the farm, cat number 1, an old black and white cat, who resides in an elevated box outside the front door. He keeps his distance though. I have been told that none of the animals are allowed in the house. Sad but true. The farm has an amusing name: Dancing Roots Farm. I put on my shoes and investigate as to the presence of another cat I have been told about, greeted along the way by the two dogs, who are wagging their tails. In the barn I find Scrumpy, who comes down the wooden stairs and jumps on me. She is a small furry bundle of black and white with a Charlie Chaplin moustache, and a motor that just purrs. I have made a new friend here.

Back inside the house, Hannah and Joan have started to cut snowflakes out of paper to decorate the formerly missing and now transplanted Christmas tree later on in the day.

CHARD

We decide on a walk outside and visit the greenhouses and fields, where greens, kohlrabi, chard, lettuce, and other winter vegetables abound aplenty. One of the dogs enthusiastically chases a pumpkin that Hannah has tossed. After many tosses it becomes somewhat more of a pumpkin fragment tossing game.

Homemade eggnog. Yum. Having forgotten the proper construction method for snowflakes, I manage to make a square one, although it's not bad, in my humble opinion. Will the other snowflakes approve? Patrick and I are drawn to the 49er–Seahawks game, which is playing on his laptop. The youth sports advertisements during game breaks are in Spanish and are repeated each time, with the same song playing in the background each time as well, reminiscent of a 70s tune. Catchy.

It's dark when Patrick and I depart to drive back to Portland to pick up some missing Christmas presents for under the tree. My navigation system (remember Schnukiputzi?) then steers us to the city of Gresham where we plan to attend the 7 p.m. Christmas Service in a Lutheran Church. It's very festive inside and packed, as churches usually are on Christmas. Wonderful old Christmas hymns fill the old wooden building, and the singers and musicians make one fall silent with appreciation. The pastor turns on a miniature pink Christmas tree and then some purple lights in quick succession before turning them out again. His sermon is about the crass commercialization and merchandising this season has become, completely forgetting Jesus, the true reason for the season. It is a memorable sermon. He concludes by saying, "Some of you have been here forty-five minutes, others ninety years. I'm happy you came." The lights in the church are dimmed and everyone gets a candle to light, passing the flame in each row, as we sing some more Christmas hymns together. I am so grateful and happy we could attend.

Across the street we pick up some eggs at the Plaid Pantry for use during the next few days, as we have run out of them. The clerk wishes us Merry Christmas, and we wish him the same back. It's so nice to hear that, instead of the silly Happy Holidays.

Returning to the farm, Patrick and I fire up the pans and cook an unusual Christmas dinner consisting of pork and chicken Schnitzel (cutlets) along with Swiss chard and mashed potatoes. Patrick also makes some delicious Rotkohl (red cabbage with apple). At the table we sample some pear brandy that Hannah's mom has brought. We decide to decorate the tree on this Christmas Eve, in the German tradition. Besides lights and snowflakes, the tree (which Patrick and Hannah cut themselves) gets some popcorn strings—that aspect definitely being an American one. Shining bright, our twinkling tree enthralls us. I receive a text message from my son Christian wishing us "fröhliche weihnachten," not capitalized but spelled correctly. Good job, my boy! I call him a bit later and find out he is having Thai food for dinner. Now that takes the cake on Christmas, so to speak. I reminisce about the superb Christmas roast beef dinners that Christian has cooked for us on many occasions prior; they are still my favorite, hands down.

We decided last night to open our presents on Christmas morning, as the Americans and French do. Hannah is exited like a little kid. She has made a beautiful leather carrying case for holding chef knives for Patrick. Patrick has given her a waffle maker, and Hannah's eyes light up. While the waffle maker is put to good use in the kitchen right away—Patrick and Hannah wearing his and hers matching aprons that Hannah's mom has given them—I pay a visit outside to Scrumpy and the dogs, bringing some leftover Schnitzel, which is much appreciated by all around. Back inside the house rather quickly, as it is still brisk outside, I decide to make Strammer Max, which consists of a pan-fried in butter slice of German bread, which is layered with Schinken and topped by a sunny-side fried egg, with a bit of salt and pepper and a cornichon. I know Hannah doesn't eat pork or beef, but since this is such a great breakfast I tell her the Schinken is really thin, trying to talk her into eating it, which sends Patrick into a laughing fit. I guess I didn't think that one through.

After our abundant breakfast, we go for another walk around the farm. The dogs are delighted, of course, but what is even more amusing is that Scrumpy accompanies us part of the way, riding first on Patrick's and then on my shoulders. Call us cat carriers, why don't you. Time for a Christmas nap. I should mention that Scrumpy has now made several attempts to come inside the house, which were denied, much to her chagrin and to my disappointment.

The kitchen has been a busy place as I come downstairs. A gingerbread house is under construction. Patrick has gone one step further and made a gingerbread outhouse, complete with a sickle moon in the door. I am put in charge of cutting tiles for the roof from flat red candy strips. The house is coming together little by little. Hannah and her mom make some Christmas trees out of candy. A gingerbread cat sits in front of the door. This has become a major construction effort.

Time for some dinner prep work. A salmon, which Joan brought down from Washington, has lain, wrapped up in a towel, in the cold entrance room that is just outside the kitchen, a place where all the farm shoes reside too. The salmon is ready to come inside to warmer climates. Patrick unwraps it, and stuffs the belly of the fish with fresh slices of lemon and parsley and tarragon collected outside earlier in the day. Two of the four big packages of kosher salt mentioned prior are now put to good use. The salt is mixed with egg whites, which bonds the salt together. Patrick then shapes the salt mass and covers the entire fish, which is sitting on a baking tray, with salt. Chard with some garlic is prepared, along with mashed potatoes as side dishes for the fish. Patrick has some trouble with the hollandaise sauce, as I think he has added too much lemon juice. But with the addition of another egg, it is thankfully saved.

It takes a chisel and dexterity to remove the salt crust, which has baked into a rock-hard mold around the fish. Inside the salt crust, the salmon, which has cooked in its own juices for the past hour, taking on the aroma of the herbs and lemons, is unbelievably moist and tender. Thank you, God, for making the fishes of the sea, and especially this particular one we are about to eat tonight.

After dinner, I walk outside into the dark to bring Scrumpy some of the salmon skin. I think I now have a friend for life. Afterwards, we all play a Scrabble-like game called Bananagrams while sitting around the dinner table. The game comes in a cloth pouch shaped like a banana. Hannah continues to amaze me with nautical terms she knows. We continue with the game Scattergories, which becomes a bit contentious after some pine brandy and loose interpretations of categories. I think it's time for bed. Unfortunately there is much barking at night once more. I suppose the dogs did a very good job of keeping away all the ferocious predators that were undoubtedly looming around us.

I put the coffee grinder to good use the next morning, now knowing the whereabouts of the coffee. Hannah and Joan are already eating breakfast, so I fix another Strammer Max for Patrick and myself. Hannah takes out some mangos and kiwis dried overnight in some sort of machine intended for this purpose. They taste very good; in fact, some of the mangos taste a bit like kiwi, and some of the kiwis a bit like mango, so I call them kangos and miwis respectively. I say goodbye to Joan, who takes off for her home in Washington State. Patrick, in the meantime, fixes me a Schnitzel sandwich to go, and Hannah adds some dried fruit to my lunch.

As I pack my belongings and open the trunk and doors of the Subie to load everything, Scrumpy manages to quickly climb inside. Patrick waves goodbye to me and then shouts "No!" when he sees the cat. OK, OK, but you do see that she wants to come. "What cat wouldn't, after all the food you gave it?" he replies. Bye, you two.

SNOW DUSTED TREES NEAR MT. HOOD

See you in a few days.

I cross a bridge near Troutdale and see fishing boats floating quietly on the river, fishermen casting their lines over the timid water on this gray clammy day. A slight drizzle ensues.

Following Hannah's written pencil and paper instruction, I find and then get to the main road near Troutdale, the one that will take me to Mt. Hood this afternoon. I turn on Schnukiputzi once again to guide me the rest of the way. As the elevation gets higher the suction cup that holds the navigation system falls off several times, due to the temperature changes on the windshield, I suppose. I get no adverse response about this from Schnukiputzi, however. I pass through a couple of towns with the very interesting sounding names of Zigzag and Rhododendron. Named after drinking a pint of pear brandy by a botanist no doubt. The pines on the mountains must have received a fresh dusting of snow last night. They look like a winter wonderland. It's a beautiful transition from green trees in the valleys to ones slightly covered with snow to the fully blanketed trees at the top of the mountains.

Mt. Hood comes into view, and after another short climb in elevation I pull into a resort-like area and enter a Visitor Information Center. After asking me, "Got four-wheel drive?" to which I respond, "Yes," the clerk tells me I need a parking pass to park at the nearby ski lodge. She draws out the route on the map and I follow her directions once I get back to the Subie. Take a break, Schnukiputzi, and you must be cold too. After several miles of driving on heavily packed snow that has been further compacted by the mountain-climbing caravan of prior cars driving on it, I arrive at the lodge. The parking lot is almost full, but I find a spot.

As I step outside the car it is cold, cold, cold indeed! I contemplate unpacking my heavy coat and a pair of gloves, which have never been used, but opt to just walk in my vest and glove-free so as to better operate my cameras. Mt. Hood is gorgeous. Patches of blue sky above, and snow abundance all around. The lower valleys have clouds and mist floating through them in ever changing patterns. It is like shaking a snow globe and then enjoying the result as the snow settles. I trudge through the snow towards the lodge, as I meet people on skis, snowboards, and snowshoes. Winter enthusiasts in bright colors. I meet a girl on a snowboard who is bent over forwards and is using her hands to walk sideways with her snowboard. It cracks me up, as I am reminded of a crab walking at the beach. She is playing it safe to be sure. I get to the lodge and walk around inside, warming up. It's a beehive of activity, with diners, hotel guests, and skiers walking in all directions. Warmed up a bit, I head out the door again and trudge past three enormous snow plows that are parked at the side of the lodge. A man is taking a picture of his family and says "cheese" to them as they pose in front of the mountain. I offer "cheeseburger," which elicits some nice grins for the picture I think. Gray petrified-looking trees pose at the edge of a snowbank. After a bit more photography, I am fairly chilled so I make my way back to the Subie, which is kind enough to respond very quickly with its heater warming up the cockpit. On my way back down the mountain I pass a closed shop that has about a dozen life-sized carved wooden bears dressed in Santa hats sitting in front of it. Rather festive, I must say.

My navigation system turns to night mode as I cover the last leg of the trip and arrive in Beaverton at my friends Patrick and Sanae's house. Merry Christmas! There is a very small Christmas tree in the front window of the living room, which I'm sure has been inspected by their cats. The house across the street has one green light and one red light on each side of its front door, and Patrick refreshes my memory about port and starboard as I comment on this light arrangement. So, for ignoramuses such as myself: red is for port, as in the color of port, or left, as in nothing left in the bottle. We exchange Christmas gifts and I am now the proud owner of some new socks to replace my holey ones, and also of a cat calendar. Patrick points out to me that their cats Mikan and Bella are featured in it. I suppose I now have to ask for a pawtograph.

We head out to dinner at their favorite Chinese restaurant, which has the all-year-round Christmas lights, where we enjoy a fine meal.

My favorite dish is the honey nut shrimp. We chat about years past, and exchange travel stories. Leaving the restaurant, I see a taxi parked next to our car. The top light says Rob's taxi. Perhaps not the best choice of names, as this may be taken literally. Coming home, I find a text message on my phone from my son Patrick: arrived? I give him a call back and then walk to the kitchen where my friend Patrick and I talk for a long time. As I talk about Calvin being at home by himself, we picture him operating the remote, watching TV, and drinking a beer. The humor progresses: what do you call a cow with two legs? Lean beef. I think it's time for bed.

I take a short walk outside up and down the block the next morning, looking at the festive Christmas decorations on the houses. A bit unexpected—a portable outhouse I pass is decorated with a large snowflake. I peruse the Oregonian over a cup of coffee after returning from the snowflake discovery, and find an article that is of particular interest. It describes the most recent cultural phenomenon in which ordinary citizens in various cities dress up in superhero costumes to help fight crime. An interesting development for the police, no doubt. Only in America, I think to myself.

Mikan has appeared in the kitchen and rubs up against me, trying to coax me into giving him his crunchies. He has limited success. Bella, the second one of the pair, makes her appearance to be petted. She has just missed the squirrel, which was sitting on top of the fence, that Sanae has put out some nuts for. Apparently Patrick is not fond of unsalted nuts, a fact that the squirrel, I'm sure, has noted with much satisfaction on his multiple returns. When the squirrel is sighted by the cats during its visits much commotion ensues, I am informed by Patrick.

"See you this afternoon," I tell Patrick, as I head to the Portland Japanese Garden, which, as you may know from my prior stories, is one of my favorite places in Portland.

There is a slight almost unnoticeable hint of rain and the sky is a slate gray. The electric cart that usually takes people up to the gardens in the summer is on a weekend schedule only during this slow time of year, and I enjoy the walk up to the garden. The garden is dry, and the trees are leafless. Only the tiniest of buds are visible on a few of the plants. Cherry and maple trees sleep, their branches visible in intricate shapes as they await spring, once again to be covered in abundant foliage. I come upon a lone camellia blossom, a bright splash of red in the monochrome landscape. I imagine what the trees and bushes might look like if they had snow on them. The main building has several Ikebana decorations in front of the large sliding doors: bamboo segments decorated with holly and white ribbons—simple seasonal elegance.

I drive by the Oregon Culinary Academy to see if they are open for a possible visit this evening, but it seems they are closed for winter break. I park downtown near the Salmon Street springs, which are dormant. It feels like winter as rain sneaks across the river. I find a hole-in-the-wall that has advertised a lunch special of meatloaf sliders. A very good special indeed, it turns out. My son Patrick starts his second restaurant job today in a Japanese restaurant. I hope it will be a good night for him. Much to learn, I'm sure.

Back in Beaverton, it's nap time. After Sanae comes home from work, we go out to a Japanese restaurant and order the bento box dinner. The waitress, who also cat-sits for them, has a minor soup spill and apologizes profusely, as is so common in the culture. No biggie, it's just soup—and good miso soup at that. I take home a small box of leftover chicken teriyaki, which I plan to airlift to Oakland tomorrow. Man, my cat sure is spoiled. We drive by the Civic Center area of Beaverton afterwards, where a huge Christmas tree in the center of a park is decorated exquisitely. Long strings of lights outline the tree. After getting home, Patrick falls asleep in his chair and I talk a long time with Sanae in the kitchen, as I won't see her the next morning.

My son Patrick calls me from the farm the next morning. I didn't realize he was still there house-sitting. We plan to meet at a restaurant favorite, St. Jack, for a late breakfast before I return his car and he takes me to the airport. I look out the restaurant window and see Patrick parking his truck kitty-corner. I'm glad the restaurant has such large picture windows to let in what little daylight there is today. It's such a contrast to the warm summer ambiance I experienced on my last trip. We split a *croque monsieur* sandwich, an avocado-egg sandwich, some *rillettes*, and of course coffee. Vive la France.

Patrick parks the truck in front of his apartment and we switch drivers in the Subie. I see his brand new acquisition: a pair of checkered chef pants. He is ready to work. He also tells me he has just purchased his own knife (to sit in Hannah's wonderful leather pouch). Good call—who knows what some of those other "house" knives have been used for. Chopping wood, exterminating rodents, cleaning fingernails—one can only ponder the possibilities. I'm happy for him, that he got this second job, with many things to learn. We say goodbye in front of the Alaska Airlines terminal. Take good care of yourself, my boy.

I manage to get on an earlier flight for a nominal fee—it beats waiting three hours in an airport. I have a nice chat on the plane with the girl sitting next to me. She is on her way back to San Francisco, where she lives, and ready to move back to Portland next weekend, where she is from, she tells me. She is wearing a hat with ears—her cat hat, she tells me. Calvin and Scrumpy would approve. She also tells me she loves watching old detective shows with her dad, and I leave her with a recommendation to watch *The Rockford Files*.

I try to catch a taxi home, but the Oakland cab drivers are giving me the runaround, telling me it costs 1/3 to twice as much as what I paid coming here. Forget it, guys, I'm not stupid. I go back to the curb and, under cover of darkness, hop into a San Francisco cab that is just unloading. The driver is perplexed and protests, fearing the ire of the local constables. I tell him to relax, that I drove taxi in SF and will back him up if he is hassled about picking up here. You just got a free paid pickup, my friend; enjoy it.

Tributes
2021

Both of my friends Big Patrick and Elvia were instrumental in the lives of my sons and I—not only expanding our culinary horizons, but also instilling a love of food and adventure in the kitchen in us. I miss them both dearly, and the following two tributes are dedicated to them.

Elvia and I had been friends for a long time. I met her around 1990 when I had a part-time job teaching at a language institute in the City. Her husband, Paulo who was teaching Portuguese at the same school, invited me to come by and have lunch at her restaurant, Café do Brasil—Brazilian Fruit Basket on 7th Street. It was a tiny hole in the wall and she was in the middle of moving to a bigger space just across the street at the corner of 7th and Mission Streets. It was there that I tasted a smoothie for the first time, long before they became popular. Elvia's smoothies were called *vitaminas*, and my sons' favorite, as well as my own, especially the banana *vitamina* which had honey in it.

As I was underemployed at the time, I offered to do some work in setting up some shelves and moving stuff in what turned into a delightful exchange of labor for food. I am not really mechanically inclined, to put it mildly, but am always willing to help. So I got to work and promptly made a couple of mistakes in cutting some wood – Manuel, the chef cooking there, started to sing a song: *"Matthias, es un hombre de papel,"* while giving me a big smile. It took me a bit, but I figured out what he had sung and I laughed, as he was absolutely right. Elvia named one of the delicious chicken entrees on her menu after Manuel, and the dish became a staple in our home cooking repertoire: chicken cooked in dark beer with plenty of spices. Later on I designed a menu for Elvia, applying some freshly learned Pagemaker skills, and thus gave credence to Manuel's song.

Café do Brasil became almost a second home for my sons and me. On birthdays, and whenever I could afford it, I would take them to lunch or dinner there, driving over to South of Market from our tiny North Beach apartment. We loved the food: *Feijoada completa* with rice, black beans, *farofa*, collard greens, and a pork chop on the side; fried bananas with cinnamon; *empanadas*; *coquinas*. Elvia's restaurant opened up a whole new culinary experience for us.

We attended the opening celebration of the new restaurant space, of course. I recall Elvia—surrounded by a multitude of helium-filled balloons—being so happy to have ample space now for cooking, and room for more customers. The restaurant was bright and airy, with picture windows on two sides. We celebrated with our favorite drink: *Guaraná Antarctica*, a delicious Brazilian soda made from the Guaraná berry.

A few years later, Elvia had to move her restaurant location again; I think she either lost her lease, or they had raised her rent. The move wasn't far, just up to Market Street—however, gritty would have been an understatement for this section of Market Street at the time (not that it has changed all that much since). But: Elvia's restaurant being there raised the bar and it became a lone bright spot between 6th and 7th Street. Inside and outside, the restaurant was painted in the Brazilian colors of bright yellow and green, and there was now also space for the occasional musical performance, or for watching soccer games. World Cup games were rather lively.

When Elvia got sick, the restaurant closed as her employees were unable to help to keep it open. It was a big loss for the many people who loved Elvia and her food, and to have a place to go where you felt welcome and were not rushed. Cafè do Brasil was so much more than just a restaurant and Elvia made sure of that.

I was able to see her in the hospital one more time, before she eventually moved back to Brazil, and thankfully she looked like she was going to be fine. In fact, she was bossing the nurses and attendants around a bit, in the manner of keeping her employees on the their toes, which made me smile. I think she was tired though, and wanted to go back home to her country of Brazil to retire, which she then did.

I love you my friend, when I come to knock on heaven's door, it would be delightful to have some *Feijoada* together. I could make some *Schnitzel* the next day too.

I named my youngest son Patrick, after Big Patrick, so in order to differentiate between the two when we got together, he was always known as Big Patrick. It was also a befitting name, as he was a tall former Vietnam Marine. I knew my friend as a chef. He learned his trade in the restaurants of San Francisco, where I first met him over 40 years ago. The restaurant he worked in that he talked the most about was Doro's, a fine high-end Italian restaurant which no longer exists. Doro's was tucked in a little alley across from the famous landmark "the pyramid," and Patrick learned to cook probably at least 20 different types of veal dishes there from the head chef, which he later incorporated into the menu of his own restaurant— as well as his own creations, of course. I think that Doro's was the restaurant that most influenced him.

If you think the Bay Area is unaffordable now, even back in 1985 Patrick decided to move with his wife, Sanae, to Portland in order to be able to afford to buy a house. This became a reality and he worked in several restaurants in Portland, plying his trade, while Sanae worked for a Japanese business. Some years later they took out a loan on their house in order to finance buying their own restaurant—a lifelong dream that Patrick had. Thus, da Vinci's Italian Restaurant was born in Milwaukie, a suburb of Portland. This was a second home to my boys and I, and we visited it almost every summer, first stopping near Whiskeytown Lake in California to go camping, which was our halfway point on the way up to Portland.

What a privilege it was to "hang out" in the back of the kitchen. Well, perhaps that is not quite the right word, because it was a tight space and when the orders came pouring in, the pace was fast and we had to duck to get out of the way of Patrick cooking at the two six burner stoves, as well as the kitchen crew buzzing at their various work and prep stations. Cramped quarters indeed.

Back in the dining room Patrick fed us his delicacies over the years: ossobuco, veal piccata, spaghetti Bolognese, halibut cheeks, and all of them came with fresh-baked garlic bread. It was a feast every time. The restaurant was kept simple in decor, with occasional dining room embellishments brought back from culinary trips to Italy. The emphasis at da Vinci's, and Patrick's view of food was to feed people—generous portions at reasonable prices. Sometimes he had specials such as abalone, and he had a waiting list for such rare culinary delicacies. Patrick just loved to talk about food all the time when he wasn't cooking. It was hard to get a word in, but that was quite OK. His stories and food knowledge were so much fun to listen to.

His drill sergeant approach in the kitchen usually weeded out lazy workers very quickly, particularly the waiters, who drew his ire more than one time. I will refrain from illustrative details, applying self-censorship here.

One of my most amusing memories was when we met up in Paris one summer for a short vacation—Patrick and Sanae on the way to a culinary exploration trip of Italy, me to see family in Germany. We enjoyed some wonderful French cuisine and had a lovely time there, however with one notable exception. One morning we sat down for breakfast in a tourist-style restaurant (we should have known better) and ordered our food. It came and was edible, but Patrick's omelet was runny. He was livid and, in colorful language, expressed his contempt for the mess in front of him, saying that this is absolute cooking basics, knowing how to cook a proper omelet. It was sent back and arrived again, this time overcooked. Patrick was ready to go into the back of the kitchen to kick the guy's butt and it took all our persuasion to have him remain seated at the table. I do believe he talked about that incident for a couple of days afterwards, and a lot in later years. It is a good thing reason prevailed; I would not have been able to restrain him physically. It showed me how seriously he took his profession.

Another time I remember well is when we went shopping together in the City for seafood in a place in the Mission District to buy some ingredients for making *paella*. As I was pointing to the various displays, and the fishmonger was scooping up mussels, clams, shrimp, and other goodies, Big Patrick subtly pointed to one of the trays on display and nudged me gently while whispering in my ear "shark," several times and grinning. The fish on the tray was labeled as swordfish. As we turned to leave the fish-monger, who somehow must have caught on to what Big Patrick noticed, removed the tray with the "shark", hopefully to label it honestly, either with the correct species, or the correct price.

Rest in peace "Big" Patrick, I love you, my friend. Oh, and you still owe me that halibut cheeks recipe!

www.ingramcontent.com/pod-product-compliance
Lightning Source LLC
LaVergne TN
LVHW010304070426
835508LV00026B/3432